OUT OF YOUR
TOWNIE MIND

—

OUT OF YOUR TOWNIE MIND

THE REALITY BEHIND THE DREAM OF COUNTRY LIVING

RICHARD CRAZE

Editor: Roni Jay

new tricks for old dogs

Published by White Ladder Press Ltd
Great Ambrook, Near Ipplepen, Devon TQ12 5UL
01803 813343
www.whiteladderpress.com

First published in Great Britain in 2004

Reprinted 2004

ISBN 0 9543914 4 6

British Library Cataloguing in Publication Data
A CIP record for this book can be obtained from the British Library.

Designed and typeset by Julie Martin Ltd
Cover design by Julie Martin Ltd
Cover image: National Railway Museum/Science & Society Picture Library
Printed and bound by TJ International Ltd, Padstow, Cornwall

White Ladder Press
Great Ambrook, Near Ipplepen, Devon TQ12 5UL
01803 813343
www.whiteladderpress.com

CONTENTS

═══

Introduction

According to recent research, as many as 40 percent of people who move out of the cities and into the countryside end up returning to the city because rural life doesn't agree with them. This is a depressing figure, not least because it doesn't have to be like that. There are lots of different ways of living in the country, and most people will thoroughly enjoy being out of the city if they can just identify the kind of country living that works for them.

This book is designed to help you find the right approach for you. We all have different dreams and different needs when it comes to the way we live. The danger is throwing yourself headlong into a new life without looking where you're going. You're almost guaranteed to come a cropper. This guide will alert you to the dangers that lie in wait for unsuspecting townies, so that you can make the move to the country fully prepared. That way, you'll enjoy it so much more, and earn your place among the 60 percent of ex-townies who stay ex.

The idea of writing this book was to analyse city dwellers' favourite dreams of country life, and to show how to avoid the pitfalls so you can make your dream come true. We ran a survey to find out what the top fantasies are – from having space and wide views, to making your own jam – and we've taken each in turn and highlighted what you really need to know. We've organised the entries in order of popularity, taking the most popular dreams first.

We also asked the ex-townies in our survey what they wished they had done differently when they moved to the country, and what they considered the biggest downsides of rural life. You'll find their answers in the survey summary at the back of the book, *What do people say about living in the country?*

PLUS ÇA CHANGE...

Looking at the responses we got from the survey, and from our own experience, there are certain overriding lessons that stand out. These general points are worth emphasising, since they apply to just about every dream and every aspect of moving to the country, so here they are.

First of all, there is the classic mistake of imagining that just because your lifestyle changes, you will change with it. It is so tempting to think that a new you will emerge from the experience of moving to the country. But it simply doesn't happen. If you're always too busy now, you'll be too busy in the country. If you're a lazy git, you'll still be a lazy git. If you're a wuss about cold weather, you'll be the same wuss only in a different place (and probably a colder one).

Now, in itself, this doesn't have to be a problem. You may be in for a bit of a disappointment when you find that inside that idyllic country cottage is the same old you that you thought you'd left in the city, but other than that it shouldn't matter. However, it starts to matter when you base your plans for your new rural life on an assumption that you are going to turn into a keen gardener, or someone who enjoys shutting the chickens in every night even in freezing rain, or the kind of person who has plenty of spare time to learn all that DIY you never got your head round before.

Many people are deeply disappointed when the vegetable patch becomes overgrown, or when they find they hate the sight of chickens, or when the kitchen still has no roof after 18 months. This is a classic mistake which is entirely understandable, and which most of us make to some degree. It can, however, ruin your dream and leave you disillusioned.

The second point is that it isn't only you who won't change. Your general lifestyle ain't going to be that different either. Messy people stay messy. Busy people go on being busy. Recluses are still reclusive. The biggest danger of all is imagining that you'll have more time in the country. But if you have a job, or a family, or a time-consuming hobby, there won't be any more free time after you've moved than there is now. Actually there'll probably be less because so many things take longer. For example, you can't just nip to the shops once you move; it may be a twenty minute drive away or more.

You may get a few weeks' lull in the usual frenetic pace of life when you first move, before you get stuck into the new job or make new friends to socialise with. But in the long run, if most of your life goes with you, most of the lifestyle will travel along too. Again, this doesn't have to be a problem. But don't plan your move in a way which relies on you having loads of free time unless you already have loads of free time. Don't take on six acres of land, or a major house renovation, or a horse, unless you would have time for it now.

Third point, along similar lines, is beware of romance that wears off. The idea of chopping logs, for instance, is wonderfully romantic. Oh, to be outdoors with an axe in your hand and the smell of freshly chopped wood. What could feel more rural and idyllic? Actually, though, when you've chopped logs every day for several months and it's now winter, you may feel differently. "Never!" you think. "Frosty evenings, chopping logs to keep warm, how could you tire of that?"

Well, that does sound pretty good. But how about freezing horizontal rain and a wind that shreds everything in its path (except the logs, which you still have to chop), and you're tired at the end of a long day but if you don't get the logs in there'll be no fire and the family will shiver all evening? Again, don't invite trouble by putting yourself in line for activities which sound romantic now but which may actually become a ball and chain.

The lesson from all this is that it's best to take the move as slowly as you can. Wait until you've been in your dream house for a few months or so before you decide whether to turn the lawn into a half acre vegetable plot, or whether to get a horse. If you're thinking of taking on a major renovation or conversion, or fancy starting a smallholding and becoming self-sufficient, take it in easy stages if you can.

You can delay launching into projects for a few months, and you can also take many things gradually, such as developing a garden or renovating a house. Or maybe you could rent for a few months before you buy, to see how you like the lifestyle and the location. Or buy somewhere easy to run – maybe small and modern – with a view to selling on and moving again when you're sure what you want.

LOCATION, LOCATION, LOCATION

And that brings me to the other significant decision you may not even realise you need to make. What sort of location do you want to be in? For example, do you want to live in a village, a small country town or right off the beaten track? There's a huge difference, believe me. Country towns have more going on, and you can be more anonymous while still getting involved where you want to. On the other hand, you won't feel nearly so connected with nature as you will elsewhere. Villages are more claustrophobic to those who don't like the lifestyle; those who do would use the words intimate or friendly. You can't hide in a village. On the other hand, if you like being involved, this is the most supportive and social kind of community to live in.

Surprisingly though, even in a small village, you won't necessarily feel close to the natural world; not unless you're right on the edge of the village or have a lot of land. The thing is, you'll open your front door onto a road or a pavement, and your immediate surroundings will either be man made or be gardens; just like in the city. The view beyond your neighbours' houses will be better than it is now – green hills and fields rather than grey shopping malls and offices – but you'll probably be in a car before you get that far from home. The village itself won't have woods and moors and open fields in it; just roads and pavements and neat gardens.

If you're not so bothered about the social side but really want earth beneath your feet and mature trees around you, with plenty of wildlife to enjoy, you need to be off the beaten track. In many parts of the country this probably only means being half a mile from a village, or ten minutes from the nearest market town, but it feels a world away.

There are countless options in between these three basic locations of town, village or off the beaten track. You could live right on the edge of a town, or a little way out of a village. The important thing is to consider the kind of location which will give you what you want in terms of amenities, views, proximity to schools and all the other things that matter to you.

If you're not sure which kind of location will suit you best, visit a few alternatives, maybe spend a few days at B&Bs in each, and think about what sort of person you are. Do you like people around you all the time? How much do you need a shop in walking distance, or a pub? Is feeling close to nature a significant part of why you want to move to the country?

Thousands of people dream of moving to the country, and with good reason. Many of them make the move and live happily ever after. Sadly, though, some find they are no happier in the country than they were in the city. Almost always, this is a result of failing to identify the potential pitfalls and think through the decisions they need to make.

This book will help you to identify the important issues, and will give you the information you need to make the right decisions. Don't abandon your dream; learn to recognise its shortcomings and find out how to enjoy it despite them. That way, the reality of country living really will live up to your dream.

—

Having space and wide views

THE DREAM

You wake early and wander downstairs with a cup of coffee and pull back the curtains. There, presenting itself in glorious panoramic vistas of magnificence is....the open countryside. The mist rises lazily off the lake; the trees are just beginning to turn gold and red and brown with the first hints of autumn cold; the sheep are grazing contentedly on grass so green it hurts the eyes and the sun is just beginning to warm the land with the first golden rays of the day. There isn't a house to be seen. There is nothing to spoil the view. There is only beauty, nature, tranquillity and space; the final frontier. This is what you moved here for. This is the dream.

THE REALITY

Well, wake up and smell the coffee because if you don't work hard, ask the right questions in advance and plan your move to the countryside carefully it ain't gonna be quite so dreamlike. Why not? Let us count the ways. That view you're looking at: first question is, 'Who owns it?' Easy answer: either you or someone else.

If it is you it means:

- Loads of money invested in buying it in the first place. Land isn't cheap anymore.

- Lots of hard work maintaining it – the countryside doesn't just happen by accident; it takes hundreds of years of careful maintenance to get it looking so neat and orderly and acceptable to us townies. Land has to be worked, you can't leave it to stand idle and empty or it will get taken over by brambles, nettles, dock and very long grass.

- If your land is to be worked, either you do it and grow old very quickly or you employ someone else to do it and they cost money. Wages aren't low in the countryside anymore; the locals also expect a decent standard of living and the old days of labourers working from dawn to dusk for a shilling, a pasty and a jug of cheap cider are long gone.

- If your land is to be worked then you are on a steep learning curve of farming practice. If you already know what you are doing then you ain't no townie and shouldn't be reading this.

- Possible taxes to pay – lots of land may mean a higher band rating for council tax and things can change at any moment. Even as we write possible council income tax is being proposed. There might be a land tax on its way – who knows?

So maybe you're having second thoughts about buying up the view. Well, here's the alternative. If the land is owned by someone else:

- You don't have control and they could edit that beautiful wood out and replace it with a cash crop of pine trees.

- They could fill in the lake and plant cabbages.

- They could fill the hillside with tents, caravans and mobile homes.

- They could turn it into a landfill site.

- You could get a mobile phone mast overnight, a pylon at any moment and a nice new town for all those townies who want to move to your special view.

Basically if you want to control the view, you also need to be able to afford it.

Next, that view which is so delightful in spring and summer turns into a sea of mud come the autumn. Rain and wind don't always enhance a beautiful view – they change it, dramatically modify it and sometimes not for the better. The word we are looking for here is *bleak*. The trees will be bare. The grass has gone. The sky is dark and rain lashed. The countryside in winter takes on a drear grey colour all over.

If you have plumped for a dramatic view and lots of space, chances are you will be miles from anywhere and miles from anyone. In other words isolated. In winter country folk don't come a-calling. They too are holed up waiting for the storms to pass. You'll see no one and go nowhere. You'd better be pretty sure you have lots of resources to fall back on. And being isolated in the country in the dead of winter may leave you feeling prey to all sorts of fears – burglars and the like. Obviously crime is much lower than in the cities but it does go on.

That's the downside. So what can you expect that's positive? Well, for a start, when the sun shines and the trees are respectfully clothed again it is beautiful. There is a sense of belonging and being part of nature that comes with the ownership of a fine view. You can waste endless hours watching the clouds scud across a perfect sky while a gentle breeze ripples the grass like sea waves. It is dramatic and inspiring. It gives you a sense of permanence and an almost religious awe at times. You can breathe easily and throw off the claustrophobia you felt in the city. The air is clean and you feel restored, invigorated and alive. Yep, space and wide views are what most people want from the countryside and they are indeed worth having. Just make sure

there aren't any planning applications in for development of a
new town before you move in.

PROS

It's beautiful.

It's the perfect antidote to city claustrophobia.

You really feel you're in the country.

It feels clean and refreshing.

You get a great view of the night sky. There are even some parts of the countryside from which you still see the milky way, unobscured by light pollution.

CONS

If you own the view it's very expensive and hard work to maintain.

If you don't own it, someone else could ruin it at any time.

It can be very bleak in winter.

A broad country view may mean isolation.

KEY QUESTIONS

II How much of a view do you want, and what do you want it to
contain?

II Do you want to be surrounded by livestock or arable farm-
land? The views are very different, and arable land can be
bleak, bare soil in winter.

II Who owns the view?

II If it's yours, how will you maintain it?

II What will it cost you to maintain it?

II What will it be like in cold, rainy weather? Maybe you should
try to see it in February before you commit to buying.

II Is it isolated? If so, how will you feel about it? If you're moving to the country with someone else and one of you is often away, how will the other one feel on their own overnight in an isolated house?

———

HEALTHY ENVIRONMENT AND FRESH AIR

THE DREAM

You move from the town to enjoy fresh air and a healthier environment and find that all your aches and pains mysteriously disappear. Colds and sniffles are a thing of the past and you feel younger, stronger, healthier. You lose weight, give up smoking, eat like a horse and walk miles without feeling exhausted. You feel rejuvenated, fresher, motivated to do more. There is no pollution and your children are safer, fighting fit and sounder in body and mind. You've all given up the junk food and being couch potatoes is a thing of the past. Yes, moving to the countryside has improved your all round health enormously.

THE REALITY

And indeed it may well be like this. But somehow we're not so sure. You see, when you move to the countryside you don't eliminate pollution, you swap it. Yes, the towns and cities are smokier, dirtier, more congested with traffic and noisier. But living in the countryside does mean you use your car more than you'd ever think. There is simply no public transport that is going to service your needs efficiently. If you run out of milk you probably have no choice but to get in your car and drive somewhere, anywhere, to get to a shop.

The countryside is not quite so fresh as you might think. Pollution knows no boundaries. It drifts over from Europe and acid rain falls where you live just as freely as in the towns. And the countryside can be unbelievably smelly. Live downwind from a pig farm and you'll know what I mean. Live near any farm and you'll be assailed by a curious mix of fermenting silage, muck (look forward to muck spreading, it really does make your eyes water), and other smells we've never been quite able to identify. We hope the farmers know what they are doing and that such a pungent whiff is absolutely essential to good farming practices but we sometimes think it might be rotting pig carcasses.

Of course once you do move to such a healthy environment you simply have no choice but to become healthier – or run the risk of immense guilt. There is a lot of pressure to do all those things you've promised yourself:

II Give up smoking

II Lose weight

II Exercise more

II Eat better (whatever that means but we assume it means give up convenience food)

II Get up earlier

II Be more energetic

II Work harder

II Drink less

II Walk everywhere

And then you move and find that all those bad habits you really believed you were going to give up have strangely followed you and you can't quite shake them off.

The trouble is that as soon as you do move, you suffer from a curious anomaly. There is no doubt that the air is fresher in the countryside, and there is simply more of it. It has an exhausting effect. Remember how you feel when you go on holiday and find you have to go to bed early because all that fresh air has wiped you out? Well, imagine what it is like to have it on a permanent basis. You simply feel worn out all the time. All those dreams and plans of getting fit, doing more, being healthier go out of the window. We're not saying don't. All we are saying is be aware that is isn't as simple as you might think. The equation *move to the country = be healthier* is a bit more complicated than it seems.

And another thing to take into consideration when moving is the weather. This has a much greater impact on your life than it ever did in the town. In the countryside the weather controls an awful lot of what you can and can't do. When it is inclement you tend to go out much less – there is nothing quite so attractive as an open fire, hot cocoa, crumpets and slippers when the wind is howling and the rain lashing and the car won't start. We all dream and imagine in our dreams that once we've moved it will always be sunny, warmer, kinder. It isn't. It will rain more, be colder and you stand a good chance of getting demotivated quite quickly if you are not really determined to maintain a fitness regime.

Isn't the idea of being snowed in romantic? It certainly is – the *idea*, that is. The reality is rather different. The appeal wears off after the first day and frustration sets in. You can't post that vital letter, you've run out of coffee, the kids are around all day because you can't get them to school…

But let's not be all doom and gloom. There are sunny spells, it does feel better and healthier. The countryside can certainly be a better place to bring up kids and to walk in. Try not to antagonise the locals too much though. In our local park it is quite a sight to see townies who have recently moved here doing their Tai Chi on a Sunday morning while the locals snigger as they make their way to the pub for their roast beef and Yorkshire pud.

PROS

The country may not be as healthy as it seems, but it's still a lot healthier than most cities.

The air feels fresher and cleaner.

It's more pleasant being out of doors in the country than in the town.

CONS

There may be less pollution in the country, but it isn't entirely absent. In the summer there's often high level hazy pollution. All year round you'll have to use your own car and pollute the atmosphere with it.

Farms are an integral part of the countryside. In children's picture books or TV programmes they're usually pretty places full of lovely animals and green fields. In reality, however, they are smelly and noisy, and a major contributor of fertilisers and pesticides.

You may tell yourself that a move to the country will mean a fresh start, and a health and fitness drive. But it's still you that you're dealing with. If you can't get round to going to the gym now, what makes you think you'll get round to going for long walks once they're on your doorstep every day of the week?

It is exhausting being exposed to fresh air on a daily basis, and it takes literally years to get over the feeling of constant tiredness and sleepiness.

Lots of fresh air means lots of weather. Well, obviously you get the same amount of weather wherever you are, but it dominates in the country. Wind, rain and cold have a significant effect on your lifestyle.

KEY QUESTIONS

Are there any major sources of pollution near the area you're planning to move to? Large farms, sewage works, factories two or three miles away in the nearest town... all of these could have a big impact on you.

II Do you imagine that you'll live a fitter and healthier lifestyle in the country? How realistic is this *honestly*? Almost no one who moves changes their approach to diet and fitness in the long term as a result.

II Would you rather be in livestock farming country (animal noise and smells) or arable land (quiet and easy on the nose, but could be full of pesticides, fertilisers and herbicides)?

II Do you want to be exposed to the elements? The more isolated you are, the more the weather will dominate your life. In the summer this is usually fine, but the rest of the year it can be exhausting and demoralising, especially if you try to fight it rather than be dictated to by the weather. Would you be happier in a small town, for example, than on an exposed patch of moorland, however beautiful the view?

II Why not get an environmental report on your proposed post-code? You can do this through a solicitor. The report will tell you about air quality, flood risk and radon in the locality.

———

THE CHANGE TO A SLOWER PACE OF LIFE

THE DREAM

What is this life if full of care we have no time to stand and stare? Well? Exactly. That's the dream. Time to chew the fat over the garden gate. Time to stop and natter as we make our purchases in the local village store. Time to stop what we are doing to watch a sunset, a rainbow, a bird in flight. Time to hold a small child's hand and dibble a stick into a pond and skim a stone on a still sea in the winter sun. Time to walk and be part of nature. Time to share with friends over long lazy Sunday lunches. Time to sit by the fire and watch the flames and dream our dreams. Time to lie in bed on frosty mornings and listen to the rooks cawing. Time to spend with family at Christmas decorating the tree and singing 'White Christmas' round the piano as the children sit and read their new picture books. Time to ....

THE REALITY

Oh do come on. There's a living to be earned. There's the chores to be done. Someone has to get those logs in before anyone can sit around warming their toes. Someone has to go to the garden centre and drag that tree back before anyone sets a single glit-

tery bauble on it. Someone has to pay for it all. Someone has to organise it all. You think that by moving to the countryside you are suddenly, mysteriously going to get another five hours a day, another two days a week, another month in the year? Well you ain't. You get the same amount of time in the country and it will actually go past faster not slower. It's a bit like getting older. When you are young you think you'll have more time as you age but then you find out you have less and there's more to do. Well, the countryside is the same.

OK, there is a type of slower pace of life in the countryside but it'll drive you mad. Round here it's called 'Devon time' (but rural areas the country over have their own version) and it means that when a builder or plumber or electrician says they will turn up on Tuesday they won't; it'll be the following Tuesday if at all. If they say it'll take three days to do a job then you can double that easily – and double it again. If they say they just have to pop out to another job then chances are you won't see them for a week. And they do all this quite oblivious to how annoying it is. You might be thinking that builders and plumbers do that in the city, but we're not only talking builders. We're talking postmen, garage mechanics, cobblers, tree surgeons, bath re-enamellers, you name it... Look, I'll give it to you straight. This slower pace of life means:

II You can't get anything done 'cos they're all so bloody slow.

II The further from a major city you are the worse it gets.

II You will keep your townie mentality for much longer than you think which means you will fume impatiently in the post office queue while we all listen to Doris tell the cashier how Auntie Mary's varicose veins are doing. Chat? Gossip? You just want a first class stamp and it takes over half an hour just to get to the front of the queue.

II When you do finally slow down and become countrified you still have to deal with people in town who haven't slowed at all which means all those deadlines are still there but you have adopted this laissez-faire attitude, mañana, and thus you get a reputation for being unreliable and the work dries up.

II You try stopping to watch a sunset and everyone else in the traffic behind you will toot and move you on. That old bugger holding up all the traffic on his Massey Ferguson tractor? He'll be the genuine article and never a townie.

II Children go at the same frantic pace whether in a city or in the countryside – they won't slow down and won't thank you for being chilled and picking them up from school late.

II Those long lazy Sunday lunches? Forget it. Everyone gets up and rushes off as they have to get Victoria to her horse riding lesson and Mark has to catch up on his homework, and your friends have their friends coming to tea and they have to rush off to bake scones.

I called the village post office the other day to ask a question about sending parcels overseas. A woman answered the phone and, when I asked the question, replied, "I don't know." I asked if she could go and find out. She replied, "Not at the moment. I'm at my lunch." In that case, I enquired, why did she answer the phone? Her response: "I'm waiting for a friend to call."

The slower pace of life is probably one of the most unrealistic dreams we townies have before we move. People in the country are friendlier and do have time to stop and chat. But they won't stop and chat to townies that often. They know we are an impatient, frantic bunch and they don't like to hold us up. Once you've made the move mentally – which takes place a long time after the physical move – you do indeed find there is time to chat more just so long as you can ease the pressure off. Don't be too impatient, it takes time to achieve.

PROS

As an outrageous generalisation, people are friendlier in the country than in the city.

If you're not in a hurry, you will find slowing down more achievable; there's less pressure in the country to get a move on.

Although it can take years to achieve, you should eventually manage to slow down. You can't rush it.

CONS

There are the same number of hours in the day wherever you are; time doesn't expand just because you've moved.

However much you may yearn for a slower pace, it's not easy to adapt. Your sense of speed is a bit like an oil tanker: it takes a long time to decelerate. If someone else is controlling the pace it's as frustrating if they're too slow as if they're too rushed.

Local country folk can drive you mad by being incapable of showing any sense of urgency (by your standards).

Other townies, by contrast, won't be nearly as relaxed as you'd like to be.

If your work keeps you in contact with the city, no one there will tolerate your slowing down or taking a more relaxed view of deadlines.

KEY QUESTIONS

II Can you say, in all honestly, that you don't get frustrated by other people slowing you down? If that city speediness is ingrained – at least for now – you're better off moving somewhere within reach of the city. They really will drive you mad in the Hebrides or on some remote Lakeland fellside. Aim for a midpoint rather than submitting yourself to virtual standstill aversion therapy.

II If you really want to move slower, and you can't expand the number of hours in the day, you'll have to remove some of the commitments. Can you do this? The shopping and the housework still take time, the school run still has to be done... if you save several hours a week by working at home instead of commuting, say, you'll have to keep them saved if you want to slow down. If you replace them with extra work, or a huge house or garden to look after, your life will be just as rushed and busy as it was before.

———

=

GOING FOR LONG WALKS

THE DREAM

*At the end of your perfect cottage garden is a little rustic gate –
painted green, made of wood, slightly in need of a coat of paint
(you know the sort of thing) – which you push open and beyond
lies the countryside. Perhaps a little leafy lane then a stile and
you're off, on a footpath that leads beguilingly through open
fields, into cool shady woods just ripe for finding truffles, mushrooms, chestnuts. The dogs are with you and the children scruffle
through leaves in their cute wellies while you stroll along behind
with your fell boots and waxed cotton jacket. Home for tea in
front of the open fire. Walking in the countryside never felt so
good, so free, so enjoyable.*

THE REALITY

It's a nice dream. It's a very nice dream. But unfortunately
unless you do some serious planning it remains just that, a
dream. John and Merry bought a delightful Georgian cottage in
a perfect location. They never gave a thought to where they
would walk, just that they would, naturally, obviously. Once they
moved in they set off on their first country walk with their dogs
and found:

II There were simply no footpaths within a two mile radius of their new home.

II The fields across which they wanted to walk were owned by unfriendly and unhelpful farmers who made it extremely clear they wanted nothing of the sort.

II Most of the fields contained animals – sheep, cows that sort of thing – and their dogs weren't that well trained and would, for safety sake, have to remain on a lead.

II They had to walk along lanes which were narrow and again they had to keep their dogs on leads as the traffic, though occasional, was fast and came up on them unexpectedly.

II The lanes were very narrow and muddy and lined with extremely high hedges which made looking over them at the wonderful view impossible and made it a bit like walking along an underpass.

The result was they ended up driving their dogs five miles away to a local common where they could run free and happily and they could get their much needed and longed for walk. Trouble is that's also where everyone else in the surrounding area walked their dogs so the longed for isolation failed to materialise – they walked with more company than they ever would have in town. Plus in town their nearest park was within walking distance. They found they were using their car much, much more than when they lived in a city.

Of course this is a worse case scenario but it did happen to John and Merry. Some townies even think that you're allowed to wander about at will over all those fields you can see from your cottage window. You do really need to check out the surrounding area before making your perfect cottage purchase. Unless you do you may find certain restrictions on your walking heaven:

II The footpaths are not as open and as accessible as you would have assumed. Sometimes it is known for them to be blocked off by barbed wire, nettles, brambles, heavy farm machinery.

II Some footpaths are deliberately kept inaccessible to discourage walkers by including a large and unfriendly bull in the landscape.

So check and check again before moving.

The weather plays a much bigger part in your walking once you've moved. In the town it's easy to put up an umbrella and walk in the park with a bit of rain but in the country the rain really does come down along with winds, mud, freezing gales and the like. Weather is much more extreme and has miles of open landscape to really get into its stride before it hits you.

Another drawback is all your townie friends will come to visit and demand a walk – it's part of the country weekend sort of thing of which you will get a lot. Now townie friends always turn up without warm clothing (who needs it in the city when there's heated taxis, central heating etc) or decent footwear. You are obliged to keep a stock of warm jumpers and spare wellies in a huge range of sizes. And they always insist on going for a walk just when you need to get the lunch on or the weather really is awful. For them it's a novelty and quite worth a soaking to experience whereas you have grown to hate it and would rather stay in and peel potatoes and listen to Radio 4 – oh, how things have changed since you moved.

Oh, and another thing. Walking in the country invariably tends to be a circular thing. You go for a three or four mile walk but for many people it always has to be the same walk because there is only one. After a year or two this can become incredibly boring – you've seen it all before – so you still pile into the car just to get a new view. In the town you often have a choice of different parks and can vary your walk so that this boredom factor doesn't kick in.

But there is an upside; there always is. If you look, you can find a new home within easy reach of accessible footpaths. You might find you have the sort of children who respond to your suggestion of a walk with enthusiasm, even joy (ha, another of your dreams eh?). You will get healthier walking more. Your dogs will have a whale of a time rolling in mud and fox shit and the like. It is quieter and safer in the country and this really is a bonus. It is also lovelier, wilder, and very inspiring. Get it right and it's fabulous. Get it wrong and it's a massive disappointment.

PROS

There are lots of footpaths in the country so long as you find the right places to look.

Many country walks are peaceful, quiet and safe.

It's easier than in town to discipline yourself to walk regularly, and it's a very healthy activity.

Many country walks are very beautiful.

CONS

A lot of country homes have a very small selection of local footpaths, and the nearest may be a car drive from your home.

Many country walks involve at least some walking on roads. These can be very dangerous — winding and without pavements — and in parts of the country high hedges will block your view. It's not what you dreamed of before you left the city.

Many footpaths are barely passable, or even totally inaccessible. Sometimes they have been allowed to fall into disrepair, often farmers make them as hard to use as possible in order to deter people like us from walking on 'their' land.

Many fields, even those with footpaths running through them, contain livestock. This can be a problem if you have dogs (a farmer can shoot a dog on sight if it's worrying a sheep). With or without dogs, not all livestock can be trusted. Although farmers aren't supposed to put dangerous livestock in fields with footpaths running through them, some still do. Sometimes they claim that the bull in question isn't dangerous at all, but do you really want to test it?

If there's only one or maybe two walks close to the house, you can get bored eventually with the repetitiveness.

Unless you are a truly dedicated walker, bad weather will get the better of your resolve to put on your boots and get out there. If you want to walk but you know deep down that you're a wuss, you'd be best off moving to somewhere like Somerset rather than the Yorkshire moors.

Once real life takes over, it can be very hard to find the time or the motivation to walk as frequently as you'd planned. The best antidote to this is a dog, which will demand that you get out every day.

KEY QUESTIONS

II What footpaths are there in the area you are thinking of moving to? (They're marked on the larger scale OS maps.)

II What condition are the footpaths maintained in? (The local Ramblers' Association can probably tell you.)

II What livestock are kept on the route of the footpaths? The sensible thing is to walk the footpaths, and then you'll get a feel for exactly what is going on. Obviously farmers move livestock around through the year, but if they're trying to deter walkers it will be obvious at any time of year.

II Some walkers are happy to fight for their rights, while other new townies in the area (blow-ins as they're sometimes known) are reluctant to fall out with their farming neighbours. If your local footpaths are difficult to use, which type of walker will you be?

II How dedicated a walker are you? Once you have the option (and indeed luxury) of walking every day, you may find that you don't exercise the option as often as you think you will.

=

Having a Big Garden

THE DREAM

You can see it now can't you? The long lawn and the huge chestnut tree with the swing hanging from it (or is it a copper beech or an oak? Hey, it's your dream, you pencil in whatever tree you want). And beyond, the vegetable garden with rows of beans, and beyond that the polytunnels housing wondrous crops of early strawberries and toms, and beyond that the wild area where the kids camp and you have bonfires and an old gypsy caravan. And beyond that? Oh, there's the wood and the stream and the couple of fields where you plan to keep horses one day, and you are turning one of the fields into a wild flower meadow.

And around the house there are huge flower borders, a conservatory, a greenhouse big enough to home a vine and a banana tree. There's a summer house and a gazebo. Why limit your dream? Have the lot, that's what I say. You might as well chuck in a folly or two, a croquet lawn, a maze and a herb garden. Oh, and what about a Japanese Zen garden? We mustn't forget that. If you have that big garden you might as well have everything you want that turns you on.

THE REALITY

Yes siree, it's a great dream full of bonfires in autumn, dewy spring days when you rush out to pick fresh daffodils from the edge of your own wood, log stores ready for the winter, ramshackle old barns full of produce wot you grew all by yourself, vast areas for the children to run in and to play outside all year round, follies and summer houses where you sit and sip Pimms as you watch the sunsets, tables and chairs left out in the dappled sunshine of big hammock-strewn majestic trees, where all your friends congregate for long dreamy Sunday lunches.

How do I know this dream so well? Why, it's one of mine of course. One I had as a small boy living in London. One I had and cherished all through my teen years. One I cultivated and watered and nourished all through my twenties. One I brought to fruition in my thirties and finally harvested in my forties. One I have had and dreamed all my life. One I now live. Hey, let me tell you what it's really like; what it's really, *really* like.

Have you any idea how much work is involved in maintaining a big garden? No, nor did I. Now I know. Now I dedicate more of my time than I ever would have thought imaginable just to trying to keep it all looking shipshape. Turn your back on any of it for a second and it grows like blazes. It grows more when it rains and that's the time you can't get out there to cut and hack and slash and mow and burn.

And it eats time. I have a living to earn. I am not retired or independently wealthy. I sit here working and watching it growing. I can either stop working and go gardening or I can stop gardening and go working. There is only that choice, no other. If I garden I lose money. If I work I lose heart. You pays yer money and you takes yer choice.

One of the most distressing things of all is finding you don't have time to maintain the garden. Unlike a building, a garden doesn't just sit and wait until you have time to attend to it. While you're trying to make time, the garden is busy filling itself with nettles and bindweed, ground elder and brambles. Your favourite alpines are being choked by weeds, and the camellias on the edge of the copse are somehow now deep inside an overgrown wood.

So you need help in the garden. Since moving to the countryside I have discovered a curious chain of circumstances. You take on a new gardener. It has taken you months to track down someone who can do anything other than mow – gardeners who can tell a weed from a prize plant aren't easy to come by. But let's say your boat has come in and you've actually found one.

They come full of energy, enthusiasm, ideas, creativity. They are industrious, invigorated and invigorating. They talk a good game. They start off fantastically. You breathe a sigh of great relief and that's when they get you. The second you relax and think you've got a good one is when it goes wrong. That shiny start dulls over. The work gets increasingly slapdash and slipshod. They don't turn up. They goof off. They let standards slip.

Before you know it the garden needs serious weeding. The gardener has to go. That's difficult enough as it is. We townies hate sacking people. We are soft and pathetic and they know it. But go they must. You cast around for a replacement. Easy? No way. Gardeners are like gold dust because everyone else is having the same problem. I think there is a hardcore of about ten of them nationwide and they are just going round the rounds. After about five years or so you end up back with the gardener you first started with.

Have you any idea what it costs to pay a gardener? Not to mention the cost of mowers, stocking that huge garden, tools (they get nicked on a fairly regular basis), weed killer, grass seed, servicing mowers and chain saws and strimmers and hedge cutters, and no, you can't do without them (and they too get nicked even if you do lock them away in padlocked sheds).

My local landscape gardener rubs his hands with glee at us townies moving in as he knows we townies all love 'projects' – putting in a pond, landscaping a rough area, creating that wild flower meadow. He was cackling the other day about a local townie who had bought two Dartmoor ponies for thirty quid each, as you do. I wanted to know why Tony thought this was so wonderful. Answer? Because the poor sod of a townie hadn't realised he had to fence in his huge garden or the ponies would wander off back to Dartmoor. He was going to have to fork out about three grand to Tony to pay for fencing. No wonder Tony was laughing.

Having a big garden is a bit like sex – you feel guilty if you aren't enjoying it all the time (or at least I do). You feel you have to get out there and eat *al fresco* every evening, spend all weekend wandering about admiring the bluebells, play croquet every afternoon while having tea in the summer house, get up at dawn every day to catch the first rays of sun as they hit the dewy lawn and you tiptoe barefoot across the grass to pick that perfect rose bud to put on the breakfast tray. Gosh, it is all so idyllic you do feel guilty if you aren't taking full advantage of it all. I'm sometimes glad when the sun goes down so I don't have to find the time to go out and enjoy it quite so much.

And the upside? Well, all the things I've mentioned. It is glorious when you finally have some time to enjoy it. It gives you a buffer zone between you and the rest of the world. It is fantastic for the children. It is wonderful for entertaining. It is beautiful and it is all mine. Would I change anything? No, never, of course not. Then why do I moan about it so much? Because I am becoming more Devon daily and we country folk like to have a bit of a whinge. You townies wouldn't understand.

PROS

You can create the beautiful surroundings you want.

It's safe and stimulating for children.

It's a buffer zone between you and the world.

A large garden is the perfect place for summer parties.

You can get out there and enjoy your own patch of countryside even when you have only a few minutes to spare.

CONS

A large garden entails a huge amount of hard work keeping it in order.

All that work takes a great deal of time. Your garden can eat up every spare minute of evenings (at least when there's any light) and weekends.

There are few things more stressful than watching your dream garden turn to weeds and brambles because you don't have time to tend it.

Gardeners are hard to come by and even harder to keep. Even people who simply mow the lawn can be deeply unreliable.

A large garden costs a fortune. It's not only the plants, and the help, it's all the equipment too.

With all that work to do in the garden, let alone the rest of your life, you may find you have very little time to enjoy the garden. This can be demoralising and may make you feel guilty that you're wasting it.

KEY QUESTIONS

II What sort of garden do you want? If you want to lay it down to lawn – or better still concrete – it won't take nearly so much work as if you want lots of flowerbeds. If you're looking at a property with a large garden, think hard about how much work it will take to maintain.

II How much time do you want to spend working in the garden? Is it your main hobby, and you're happy to put a couple of solid days' work into it every week, or do you just want to spend an afternoon a month tidying it up?

II How do you cope with a garden that is getting the better of you? Do you burst into tears at the sight of a weed, or do you rather like nettles for their wildlife value and take a sanguine view of nature overrunning corners of your once well-tended plot?

II How do you feel about having a gardener? Can you afford one? Are you happy to have someone else wandering around your garden curtailing your privacy much of the time?

II Gardeners tend to cost between about £5 and £10 an hour, depending on whether they're a local teenager who just mows or whether they are skilled, professional weeders and pruners. Are they easy to find in the area you're thinking of moving to? It might be as well to ask around, maybe at the local post office or village shop.

II What is a large garden going to cost you? You really need a decent lawn mower – probably a ride-on – if you have a lot of grass to cut. Then there's the strimmer, hedge-trimmer, chainsaw, shredder... not to mention all the usual tools. And the plants, of course. You may be taking over an existing well-stocked garden. But if you're planning to create flower beds and shrubberies from scratch, look round a garden centre and check out bulb catalogues to get an idea of price. We could be talking literally thousands of pounds.

II Will you resent the lack of time to sit and enjoy a garden that takes all your free time to maintain? Some people love working in the garden and are happy to have the chance. Others believe gardens are for relaxing in. If you're in the latter camp, you may feel you're wasting time tending a garden that you'd rather just sit back and look at with a gin and tonic in your hand.

BEING PART OF A COMMUNITY

THE DREAM

You sit on the tube or the train or the bus – or even in the traffic jam every morning – staring at faceless strangers. Your eyes slip past them. If only you had the time to stop and chat. If only you knew your neighbours. If only you could leave your front door open and have friends pop in. If only the local amenities were run by friendly faces that you knew. If only the carol singers who came round at Christmas were smiling and cute and you didn't fear being mugged by them. If only you could get involved in the local activities – organising bonfire night celebrations or being the neighbourhood watch rep. In short if only you lived in a caring, supportive community where everyone knows everyone else and looks out for them. If only you could experience a true sense of belonging. If only you could feel a part of a real rural community. Wouldn't it be nice? Wouldn't it be fab?

THE REALITY

Actually no, it wouldn't. Well, in theory it can be, but the reality is a wee bit different. For a start you will quickly get bored seeing those familiar faces every day. And that's every single day. There is no escape. You can't suddenly trade them in when you feel a bit fed up with them. They are there for keeps. They don't move away. They don't move on. They stay. And you never chose them in the first place – you won't even like some of your neighbours. I know someone whose local born and bred neighbour threatened him with a shotgun for daring to exercise a perfectly legal right of way across his land, and he still had to live next door to him and mix in the same group of people at village events.

Your neighbours, what is more, will be more than happy to see you every day (assuming you haven't committed any of the cardinal sins listed below, or tried to exercise a right of way across their land). They will love to stop and chat every day. What about? Oh, let me see. The weather. Your neighbours. What was on telly last night. A bit more about the weather, and what they might be having for their tea. And that is it. Every single day. Without fail. Come rain, come shine. That is about the limit of it.

And what else is a wee bit unrealistic about your dream of living in a rural community? OK:

II Those familiar faces will all, pretty well, be the same colour. Invariably pink. There is little in the way of a racial melting pot in the countryside. This isn't a good thing or a bad thing. It is just a thing. You may quickly miss the cross-cultural mix you get in a city – or in any decent sized town. Look, let's be honest here: if you belong to any sort of 'minority' be it racial, sexual or religious then the chances are you won't be greeted with such completely open arms as you might like to think. This isn't cruelty but ignorance; many country folk have no experience of your particular existence and thus they will be naturally resistant.

II It is their community you are buying into. They will have their own rules and you will be expected to slot in quickly. If those rules involve knowing everything about you, your business and your habits then you'd better be ready to be completely open or they will think you stand-offish. I knew a woman once who lived in a very small village and was very private, preferring to keep herself to herself. She was known locally in the village shop as 'that single woman with the cats', always said in a very disapproving way. It was all they knew about her and they made it sound as if she was a Satanist.

- Other townies. Small communities attract lots of townies – you're ready to go yourself so you understand this attraction. Before you know it the whole place is jam packed with sloanies and dinkies and nimbys and the verges are being mowed and the place tidied up and speed humps put in and the cockerels silenced. The locals have all moved out and you might as well be in a town for all the community spirit there is left.

- Interference. The members of your new community have been there a long time – the locals were probably all at school together – and have been used to doing things their own way for a long time as well. They won't thank you for suggesting changes; nor will they be happy if you don't go along with the way they do things. They certainly don't want you to come in and take over their organisations (that's how they'll see it), from the village fête to the weekly pensioners' shopping trip. You may think you're helping; they won't. On the other hand, *they* may well like to interfere – they call this giving advice – and you won't be able to prune a hedge without some or all of them dropping by to tell you the right way to do it 'round here'.

- Lastly, local communities can be very old fashioned – they need dragging into the twentieth century, never mind this one – and you will be expected to shop in a village shop that is expensive and badly stocked. You will be expected to enjoy junk food at community events such as bonfire night. And you will be frowned on if you drive a modern car, eat guacamole, read any broadsheet newspaper apart from *The Daily Telegraph*, wear 'fashion' or have a Filofax. Many city habits are totally alien to country folk too. Try to foist any of them on your new neighbours and you will be immediately ostracised, outlawed, alienated, frozen out. Know what I mean? Loud music late at night, friends who reel home roaring drunk, wandering around naked with the curtains open… keep your modern city ways to yourself for a while or they'll simply stop talking to you. What happens then to your sense of belonging?

Sounds dreadful doesn't it? Well, it can be if you get it wrong. But get it right and it is genuinely fabulous. I know. I have a local community that is supportive, caring and encouraging. They walk my dogs when I can't. Take in the milk when I forget. They allow me privacy but are ready to stop and chat when I need to. Many of them are forward thinking and modern although they still use quaint expressions such as 'dimpsy[1]', which make me laugh, but are happy to explain what they mean without patronising me. It gives me a really warm feeling to belong to a community that I wasn't born into and one that looks after me so well. I am happy.

You can certainly increase your acceptance into the local community by joining local groups such as the amateur dramatics, the local branch of the RSPB, a running club or whatever. Just make sure you don't put their noses out of joint by trying to take over.

PROS

It gives you a great sense of belonging to be surrounded by people who actually know your name and who you are.

If you tread carefully, you can become involved in plenty of community activities, and volunteers are always needed to run the coffee stall or drop copies of the parish magazine through letterboxes.

In a strong community, you will be surrounded by supportive people who will keep an eye on you and your property, and give you help when you need it. Obviously you'll have to respond in kind, and this will make you feel that you matter.

---

[1] Twilight – as in 'tis getting dimpsy now'.

CONS

In the city you may not know your neighbours, but this can be an advantage. They might be ghastly. At least you don't have to talk to them. In a small community, life can be pretty unpleasant if you fall out with your neighbours so you need to make an effort. But country neighbours can be just as ghastly as city neighbours.

If you're not a white caucasian heterosexual you may encounter a level of resistance you never expected. Country folk with little experience of other lifestyles and cultures can be an intolerant bunch. Often they soften with time, but you may neither want to wait, nor see why you should have to.

That anonymity you find uncomfortable in the city can seem like a far-off luxury once you're in the country. You simply won't be used to the invasion of privacy that passes for concerned interest in a rural community.

Your fellow townies are sods for messing up your dream of country living. Just as you're enjoying the wildness of the countryside, they come along and tidy it up, mowing everything and cutting the hedges in June so the improved visibility will make the roads safer — even though it kills off all the wildlife you moved here to enjoy.

You may want to get involved, but unless you tread very carefully you'll make enemies you can ill afford. The community will feel very threatened if they think you're interfering or trying to take over their systems and institutions. It will take years to become sufficiently accepted to put yourself forward for any of the important jobs, such as chair of the village fête committee, without putting backs up.

In the city, you can live pretty well however you like and people leave you alone. You may feel isolated by other people's lack of interest in you, but at least you're free to enjoy your chosen lifestyle. In the country, by contrast, nobody likes a nonconformist. Small communities don't have room for them without threatening their identity, so they don't welcome different behaviour.

KEY QUESTIONS

II What size community will you choose to live in? This is a very important point to consider before you move. To many people, a small village seems like the ideal rural community. For some people it is, but it is also the most claustrophobic, the most intolerant and the least flexible. Unless you're happy to take a back seat for several years, without being too private or non-conformist, you may find it difficult to fit in. A small country town can accommodate more variety if you are in any way 'different'. Or an isolated spot with few neighbours may be ideal if you're fairly private. There's less to get involved in, and a neighbour dispute can be very unpleasant, but if you're a good diplomat and want to keep to yourself it can work very well.

II What are the neighbours like? The smaller the community, the more important this question is. If you find a property you like, why not knock on a few doors and say hello. Try asking each person what the neighbours are like – you'll soon find out if they're a supportive group of friends or a warring collection of troublemakers.

II Will you be accepted by these people? If you're openly gay, or have green hair and pierced nipples, you could find that country folk look askance at you. You'll have less difficulty in rural communities close to cities where there's a large ex-townie contingent already. And, perversely, you can be better off in a real backwater where people expect all outsiders to be weird anyway.

II Do you want to live among real dyed in the wool country people, or would you rather have a few townies around? You need to check out the community you're moving into if you have a preference. Ask around; as always, the village shop or post office is the fount of all knowledge.

II Are you hoping to get involved in organising and helping at events? You need to recognise that you'll have to take this slowly or barriers will go up. The larger the community, the greater the scope for getting involved. Villages are busy places; in a small country town you won't get to know everyone but you'll be more able to get stuck in to organising events without putting noses out of joint. You may even get away with launching a new event or local organisation, which you certainly won't be able to do in a small village for several years.

II What groups exist in the village, town or area for you to get involved in and start getting to know the community and feeling a part of it? Some communities are far more active than others; if this is important to you, find out how busy they are in the area to which you want to move.

=

Being near trees and wild flowers

THE DREAM

You sit in your dark office dreaming of views of woods, forests, wild flowers, sunlit glades, dappled meadows, streams with banks lined with native plants and alive with insects. The names come to you – cow parsley, wood vetch, goosefoot, dodder, toadflax, willowherb, primrose, cranesbill, sea pinks, campion, marsh marigolds, rosemary and fat hen. And the trees, ah, the trees. Oak and beech, birch and the lovely silvery mountain ash. Chestnuts and hazels, hornbeams and maples, planes and poplars, sycamores and willows. And let's not forget the elms, trees of dreams indeed. And all this is available to us the second we move. All this glory, this beauty, this heaven of nature's creation.

THE REALITY

Yes, it is all available but it does come at a price you know. Quite a heavy price if you want to know. You don't? Then your dream might be a disappointment. Better to be a bit realistic and then the dream will live up to expectations. So what are the drawbacks of being near trees and wild flowers? Surely there can't be any? Surely this dream is so simple it has to come true? Well, you might think so but there are drawbacks. Here they are:

II Trees don't just grow. They also have to be owned. If it is you who owns them then you have to maintain them, and cut them up when they fall down in storms and block your neighbour's drive. Woodlands have to be managed. If you don't own them you have no control over them and they fall down over your drive or just simply disappear overnight (OK, they don't really disappear, farmers cut them down).

II And you can't necessarily just cut them down. If you own them they may have tree preservation orders (TPOs) on them; touch them at your peril. It's just other people's that don't have TPOs, and they're the ones you love best and then they get the chop.

II Trees produce waste products – leaves. These block your gutters every autumn. They fall into your swimming pool/pond etc and rot down to a lovely grey smelly sludge as soon as your back is turned.

II Trees can cause subsidence if they are too close to the house. Their roots form a wonderful tangled web that stops you laying pipes easily underground.

II Trees too close to the house also make it dark and damp, dank and dreary.

II Wild flowers produce wild seeds. These find their way into your lovely cottage garden and before you know it you're producing more dandelions than dahlias.

II Fever. Yes, fever. Have you any idea how many townie friends have hay fever? What a palaver. Now don't go thinking I'm unsympathetic (well, actually I am) but they sneeze and clutch hankies and claim they can't go outside where all those wild flowers are. They say the word 'wild' as they would use it to mean wild animals – not merely natural but somehow escaped, dangerous, untrained and untameable.

II A lot of wild flowers produce extremely dangerous seeds – poisonous. Think hemlock here, think dog's mercury. Sorry, what am I thinking of, you're a townie and probably haven't a clue, like me, what is and what isn't poisonous. Best treat it all as dangerous until you know better. And it's not just the seeds but also the sap, the flowers, the stems. Add to this the stinging and scratching varieties, and the fact that all these attract stinging and biting insects, and you need to keep your wits about you looking after small children.

II Does your dream property have hedges? Hedges need cutting, and finding someone to do it can be a problem. Local farmers have their own hedges to cut and often say they'll cut yours in the summer, when they get round to putting the flail on the tractor for their own hedges. By October there's still no sign of them and your neighbours are complaining to you that the branches from the hedges are scratching their cars. When the farmer finally turns up, he has to be paid for the job of course.

Trees can also be noisy, although I can't quite bring myself to list this as a drawback. Near us is a stand of very large beech trees. Lovely to look at but the cawing that comes from them every morning and evening as the entire flock of rooks (sorry, let's get it right, the *parliament* of rooks, see what a townie I am) takes to the skies and wheels overhead for up to half an hour screaming at nothing in particular. Now don't get me wrong. Rooks is romantic. Rooks is what the countryside is all about. But rooks is also about not being able to hear yourself think twice a day, everyday. Rooks is romantic but wrong.

Gawd, I do hope we haven't put you off too much. Trees and wild flowers are actually fab. The upside is that they are beautiful, wondrous, inspiring, relaxing. They allow you freedom and they are educational. They bring you closer to nature – they *are* nature. They put you in touch with the seasons and they make you fall in love with them. I wouldn't change any of it. I even love the rooks and would miss them desperately if they didn't drive me mad twice a day.

PROS

You never tire of looking at trees and flowers. They change so much through the seasons that they are a continual pleasure.

Trees can help give you privacy and seclusion, and in some areas act as a valuable windbreak.

Being near trees and flowers makes you feel part of nature and is what moving to the country was all about.

CONS

Trees have to belong to someone (it doesn't seem right, but they do). If they're yours, you have to maintain them. If they're not yours, you have no control over whether they stay or go. If there's a TPO in place, you don't even have the right to cut your own tree down.

Deciduous trees close to the house mean endless gutter clearing (and pond/pool/lawn clearing too).

Large trees close to the house or garden walls can cause structural damage as they grow.

Summer shade is lovely, but too much of it can be claustrophobic. You don't want to cut off most of the natural light in the house, or have a garden you can't sunbathe in.

Wild plants near your flower garden are an uncontrollable source of constant weeds.

Wild flowers are bad news for hay fever sufferers.

Many wild plants are dangerously poisonous; a particular concern if you have children.

Hedges are a hassle to get cut, and it will cost money.

KEY QUESTIONS

II How close to your dream property are the neighbouring trees?

II Who owns them?

- How large are they, and will they affect the house or your ability to lay pipes and cables nearby?

- Is any of them subject to a TPO?

- If you view your house in winter, how much shade will the trees cast in the summer? Will they make the house dark or the garden too shaded?

- If you view your house in summer, what view will you get in winter when the leaves have gone? The trees may be sheltering you from an unpleasant view of the local power station, or giving you privacy in summer that will be lost in winter.

- Is any of the flower beds close to wild flowers or fields? Are you prepared for all the extra weeding this can entail?

- Do you suffer from hay fever, or do any of the family or frequent visitors?

- Will you have a lot of hedges to cut? What will it cost and where will you find someone to do it?

———

=

BEING NEAR WATER

THE DREAM

Imagine. It is dawn. The lesser-feathered hoot calls forlornly across the marshes. The tide is out and the mudflats are alive with waders and dippers, catchers and plungers. Just out there, where the little waves lap, a small boat is moored, waiting. It is your boat. All you have to do is slip the oars, cast off and you'll be away, out into the bay, out into freedom. There is a little light mist rising and not a soul around to spoil this perfect dawn on the river; this perfect day by the sea. Overhead a heron glides majestically as it comes in to land light as a feather on the edge of the water where it feeds greedily. You hoist your one red sail and slip silently out into the main channel. You pull the collar of your midshipman's jacket up higher as the morning air is still cold but you feel alive, happy, content, smug. This is the life, messing about in boats, fishing, or just sitting and gazing.

THE REALITY

The dream can sometimes live up to the reality but often it doesn't because the reality has something missing, or has an extra something that we didn't take into account. I once took a young son of mine on a ramble along the sea shore and he seemed mis-

erable and fed up. We did catch sight of a cormorant but that wasn't enough. He finally admitted he was disappointed as there was no music. And it was too windy. He was too used to watching nature programmes on the telly where you did get music and it was never windy.

So what's missing from our dream of living near water – and what's extra that might piss on our fireworks? Well, for a start living near water does mean it is damp. Now that's fine in the summer but come the winter it gets to be a real problem. How close to water you are will determine whether you run a serious risk of flooding. Some areas are particularly prone to flooding, and yet townies often view properties in summer and don't even check. One of our local villages has a banked up river, which floods every winter without fail, and alongside it there is an old terrace of cottages built below the level of the banks. The amazing thing is that people actually buy these houses, and then complain to the council when they flood.

A friend of mine had a country house once which had the river running through a culvert underneath it. Yes, it flooded every winter but there were flagstone floors and the water came in through the front door and out through the back door. Upstream they once had a yellow plastic duck race. They let hundreds of these ducks go, each with a number attached to its back. They promptly disappeared under the house and vanished. The organisers sent down a diver but he was unable to locate the missing ducks. Eventually after a week or two one bedraggled duck did reappear and someone was voted the winner. That winter, as the river levels rose, you could hear the ducks bobbling about in the brick culvert under the house when it was very quiet in the early hours of the morning. Quite eerie. Come the spring when the levels went down sufficiently they did all, one by one and very mildewy and decrepit, reappear but there was no one there to see their triumphant emergence into the sunlight once more.

On the Somerset Levels (and no doubt certain other places such as the Fens) the houses were designed to flood in winter. This went on as late as the mid 20th century, until the area was drained. As the weather turned in the autumn, all furniture and rugs were taken upstairs, where the family moved to for the duration. I once read an interview with a chap who had grown up like this. They used to moor their boat (their only transport) to the banisters, and fish for their supper from the landing. It wasn't hugely healthy, but they managed fine. Little surprise, then, that many houses on the Levels still flood every winter.

However, many houses which flood are impossible to sell. In areas where flooding is a worry, houses can sit on the market for years after flooding perhaps only once, many years ago. (Until a townie comes along, of course.)

Living near water often means you gain a lot of fair weather friends. They come down for the boating or the swimming or the beach parties when the sun is shining but you won't see 'em in the winter. (This, mind you, might be regarded as a bonus in some cases.)

We often make assumptions about what we are going to do to live out our dream without taking into consideration that everyone else might well be wanting to live out the same dream. I moved to Devon to be near water – the river Dart – and quite naturally bought a boat and expected to be able to rent a mooring locally. I was told I would have to wait for *dead-man's moorings*. Yes, you have to wait until someone literally dies for a mooring to become available. I bought a smaller boat which I tow to the water when I want to use it.

Oh, and another quick word about keeping boats. The amount of time you get to use them is much less than you would ever think and the amount of money you get to spend on them is much more than you'd ever think.

Whether you want to boat, fish, or sit by the river bank in the early evening, you won't be alone. Lots of wildlife also loves liv-

ing in or near water – mosquitoes, midges, sea gulls (you have no idea how raucous and destructive they can be) to name but a few. The more boggy or wooded your stretch of river bank, the worse it will be for midges.

Perhaps you don't want rivers and lakes. Perhaps your dream is to live by the sea. Long walks on the cliffs, collecting driftwood along the tideline, skinny dipping at midnight. All of this is wonderful, but there are still downsides. If you live near the coast it can be pretty bleak in winter. The weather whips across, the rain drives at you and the view is grey. Beautiful and inspiring for a weekend maybe, but for months on end? You can't even get from the house to the car without getting soaked and frostbitten. Day after day after day. And the wild weather plays havoc with your garden. All that salt in the air means your choice of plants is severely limited. Fine if you're not a gardener, but depressing if you are.

But living near water is fun, beautiful, cathartic and ever changing. It is uplifting and relaxing, and there is *nothing* – absolutely nothing – half so much worth doing as simply messing about in boats. Whoops – a bit of personal bias creeping in there. OK, maybe for you fishing or sunning yourself on the beach are closer to your watery ambitions. But whatever your dreams of water, they can come true if you're wise to the drawbacks.

I know someone who reckons that the best way to live near water is to live on an estuary. This makes a lot of sense. You're protected from the harshest seaside weather, but you're bound to be close to the sea. The wildlife and the view is extremely varied and always present, and you can boat, fish or enjoy whatever riverside activities you please.

PROS

If you enjoy fishing, boating, swimming in the sea, cliff walks or other water-related activities, they'll be right at hand if you live near water.

The wildlife and the views are inspiring and relaxing to enjoy.

You'll attract lots of visitors (if that's what you want).

CONS

Flooding is a significant risk in many properties near water. And, to add insult to injury, insurance can be expensive or even non-existent in high flood risk areas.

Even if it doesn't flood, it's generally damp. This may affect the house, or you may find damp weather affects your health.

Boats are expensive, and if you don't have your own mooring you can't assume that there'll be one available nearby.

If you fish, you may find that you get less time for it than you hoped. And you can't simply set up your rod and fish anywhere — you have to have a licence or a right to fish any particular stretch of water.

Not all the wildlife is fun.

Living by the sea can be terribly bleak and cold in the winter.

Salty air by the coast makes gardening extremely challenging, and many of your favourite plants may simply refuse to grow.

Living anywhere near water is always dangerous if you have small children, elderly folk or non swimmers. You cannot relax for a moment if the river runs through your property or the sea comes up to your front door.

You have no control over what other people put in the sea or rivers. You can't assume any water will be safe or clean, and in some cases you can be quite sure it isn't. In some areas, Weill's disease is a significant risk.

KEY QUESTIONS

⁏ Do you want to own a stretch of water, or simply have it in your view? Or merely be in reach of it, such as a close drive to the sea?

⁏ If you want to be by the coast, can you cope with the bleakness

in winter? How long is winter in the part of the country you're looking in? Would you be better off a few miles inland?

II Is your dream property likely to flood? Badly? Will you be able to get affordable insurance?

II What are your water-related hobbies? Boating? Fishing? Check out how much these will cost, and whether you can easily get access, mooring rights, a fishing licence or whatever it is you need.

II How do you feel about mosquitoes? Most of us wouldn't cancel the dream of living near water just to avoid midges, but it might put you off buying somewhere right on the water's edge. Perhaps you'd be better off with a house a hundred feet up the hillside.

II Are you a keen gardener? Will you be able to grow the plants you want to near the sea, or in boggy ground?

II Is safety around water an issue in your household – are there children or non-swimmers? This may affect how close to water you choose to be.

———

SOMEWHERE SAFE TO BRING UP KIDS

THE DREAM

We've all seen those lovely Edwardian illustrations of kids shrimping or climbing trees or just running carefree across fields of poppies and buttercups. Or we imagine our children free-wheeling their bikes down leafy lanes and across a tiny stone bridge where they fish in ice cold streams for tiddlers which they bring home in a jam jar to a slap up tea. I grew up on the Famous Five and I say, well, crikey, it's all such blinking good fun, gosh. Camps in the woods. Cooking breakfast outdoors over an open fire. Scouts and Guides. Flying kites and whittling wood.

THE REALITY

Yes, a dream anyone with young children might have. We want them breathing fresh air. We want them safe. We want them growing up hale and hearty, healthy and happy. We want them to know their neighbours and trust strangers. We want a 1950s upbringing for them but can we turn the clock back? Can we recreate that ideal?

Imagining that the second we move to the countryside all our

problems and all the problems of a modern world are going to evaporate is, I'm afraid, a bit of a romantic notion. You may solve some problems but you will replace them with others. Crime isn't non-existent in the country. It may indeed be greatly reduced but it still exists. Not all country folk are friendly smiling ruddy faced yokels. There are inner city areas in big country towns and sink estates in country cities. You may escape the rat race but you're probably only swapping black town rats for brown country ones.

Is it safe for children? Yes.... and no. There are dangers in the countryside. Let's take farms for instance. They're everywhere in the country and they certainly aren't safe. There aren't too many silos and combines, chemicals and slurry pits that would pass the health and safety inspections that apply to city parks and playgrounds. Climbing trees in the woods may seem a safe activity but again it would require bump proof matting to be laid, a trained and properly qualified first aider on site, adult supervision, no climbing above two foot off the ground, insurance and any choking hazards such as leaves to be removed beforehand.

Then there are the rivers and leats, drainage ditches and dew ponds, lakes and haystacks (they catch fire and/or fall on you), cow related incidents (people get gored, trampled, butted, trodden on, chased and tossed) and snakes (rare but there are more adder bites in the country than in the city), railway lines and cave systems, cliffs and escarpments. Need I go on?

In the countryside there are fewer activities for children which means you end up endlessly driving them everywhere to whatever is on offer. The longer you spend in a car on fast country roads, the more prone to accidents you are. And all those dreams of cycling to school won't happen – too muddy, too dark in the mornings in winter, too far, too dangerous, too everything.

You have to drive your children around because otherwise they get bored. Children that move young will be happy in the woods and fields, most of the time, up to their teens. Teenagers who are forcibly relocated will almost all find the country terminally boring. But even those who grow up there want more by their teens – cinemas, shops, you name it, it's all a car journey away at least.

Just because you have a house that looks out over fields, that doesn't mean you're allowed to use the fields. If you want your kids to play in the countryside, what access will they have to it? You might aim to buy a place with a couple of acres of wood and a paddock, or maybe opt for a house close to a common or near footpaths. But don't assume that just because the countryside is on your doorstep you can necessarily step out into it. I know plenty of children who can't actually get at the countryside beyond the back garden unless their parents put them in a car and drive them there. You can do that in the city (although the journey will be shorter in the country).

We also think that moving to the countryside means we go back in time. Back to a time when drugs didn't exist. But drugs have always been around and they are as freely available in the country as they are in the town (or so I've been told). And the same goes for pubs and, in fact, anything that is going to lead your delightful darlings astray. If they are going off the rails they'll do it just as easily here as in a city.

But, and this is a big plus, at least you'll know the parents of the kids who are selling substances to your kids. You'll know everyone actually. And you'll learn who to trust, who to hang out with, who is cool and who isn't.

Your kids will be safer in the countryside if *you* do your job properly. They will lead more energetic lives, be fitter and healthier (or not depending on how much *you* allow them to get away with), walk more, watch less TV, eat better (again it's what *you* give them to eat that makes the difference). People will look out for them, bring them home when they get drunk in the village pub and they will grow up with a caring and supportive network of close friends.

PROS

Kids that grow up in the countryside can easily be encouraged to appreciate nature, to build dens, to fish, and all those other activities you dream of for them.

Although children are no safer from strangers in the country than in the town, there will be far more people around who aren't strangers and who will look out for them.

The air is fresher and the atmosphere mostly cleaner.

CONS

The countryside is no playground. It's full of health hazards for children. You have to keep them off farms and away from water, and then trust to fate to keep them safe when they're up trees or building dens.

The roads are often far more dangerous than in town: the visibility is poorer and the cars go faster.

Children can get very bored in the country, and need to be ferried everywhere. There's generally no other means of transport but you.

Dangers such as drugs are just as prevalent in the country as in the city.

KEY QUESTIONS

II If you already have children, how will they feel about moving to the country?

II What will they do in their free time?

II How much access will your children have to the countryside?

II How much of a free taxi service are you prepared to be? If you're not prepared to ferry your children around constantly, what other transport is available?

II What are the dangers near your dream home? Water? Nearby farms? Roads or railways?

GROWING YOUR OWN VEGETABLES

THE DREAM

Simple. Rows and rows of freshly grown organic vegetables. Sown by the light of the moon and harvested at dawn. Companion planting of flowers and herbs. Polytunnels stocked with spring tomatoes. Acres of new potatoes. Banks of salad crops. Orchards of apples. Greens and reds and golds and browns. Fresh crunchy crops picked as you need them for glorious Sunday lunches. Huge marrows entered in the local village competition where they win first prize. Neat wigwams of runner beans. Beds and borders fringed with brick paths. Orderly squares of greenery and freshness and lushness. Perfect weather.

THE REALITY

This is a dream I had. I fled the city. I bought copies of *Self Sufficiency*. I watched *The Good Life*. I bought an acre garden and hired a rotovator. I hoed and planted and dug and seeded and weeded. I pored over catalogues and selected the best – *Summer Gold, Farmer's Delight, Autumn Reds, Spring Harvest* – and waited excitedly for them to be delivered. I followed the instructions. I drilled and trugged and dibbered and thinned. I netted and protected, watched over and watered and loved and cherished. I poured my heart and soul and blood and guts into that garden. It was my dream.

I got backache and tears and the birds got most of what was left after the chickens got out and scratched up the rest. I was undeterred and planted again. The frost got the next lot. Again. Rain and flooding. Again, come on, bring it on. Too hot a summer and a hose pipe ban. Again. Now I'm out there challenging the forces of nature, ranting, bareheaded, mad, shaking my puny fist at God. Last time, I swear it, last time. Again. Slugs. I retire hurt. Score? Nature 6. Townie nil.

I look over the fence at Old Joe's garden. It is the dream come true. Old Joe thinks I'm funny. Old Joe has been at this game for over fifty years. He gives me vegetables to cheer me up. Luscious leafy organic fresh plump vegetables. Great. How do I feel now? I buy Old Joe a drink in the village pub and he regales the locals with tales of all my doings in the garden. They roar with laughter. Oh, those townies are so funny aren't they? I buy them all a drink.

I try fruit next. Soft fruit gets eaten by birds. Hard fruit rots in tights. What? I read in one of these books for townies that apples can be stored wrapped in newspaper or an old pair of tights. You drop an apple into the tights then tie a knot, then another apple etc until the tights are full. Result? Apples wrapped in newspaper all went rock hard and inedible. The ones in tights went soft, putrid, rotten, and inedible.

Tried peas. Birds got them all. Tried flowers: greenfly. Tried strawberries: slugs again. Tried chickens: rats got the eggs, chickens got the vegetables. Retired hurt. Went back to the city to lick my wounds. Went back to the country many years later and bought vegetables and fruit and eggs and flowers from supermarket. Much more like a country person then than ever before.

I've known townies have the 'grow your own vegetables' dream and do it very successfully. Perhaps it is just me. They seem to be able to have polytunnels full of lovely grub. Mine collapsed in the first strong wind. They plant rows and rows of beans and get rows and rows of beans. I planted and got sickly seedlings. What's the opposite of green fingers? Townie thumbs? I've got 'em.

I find now that most townies who make the move and grow their own stuff were doing so already in the town albeit in a tiny back yard or in pots on the window sill or on an allotment. Those who weren't growing veg in the city are unlikely to do so successfully in the country. It's to do with experience and aptitude and motivation. If you are going to have a go then do it properly. Get some training, talk to others who do it successfully, read up on it in magazines and books, enrol on a course, do a few weekends practising – try *Working Weekends on Organic Farms*, that sort of thing first.

Assuming you do manage to get the crops to grow, it's an awful lot of hard work. To produce more than half a dozen meals' worth of vegetables a year, you really have to put in plenty of hours, some of them in foul weather. Unlike keeping a rockery or growing a rose garden, vegetables are not only time-consuming but also require masses of spadework and hard physical labour.

And when the vegetables finally come along, they're like buses: they all come at once. You have to eat nothing but runner beans for about six weeks in the summer, then force down courgettes until you feel sick, or binge on lettuce for months on end. Eating food in season is great, but eating it to the exclusion of all else can be pretty tough going. And don't think you can fob them off on your neighbours; they're all desperately trying to get rid of *their* excess. By August the whole village will be sneaking around before dawn leaving little anonymous bundles of courgettes and tomatoes on each other's doorsteps in a bid to offload the surplus.

But if, unlike me, you manage to grow good crops there is nothing more satisfying than picking your own vegetables, harvesting your own fruit. I know now. No, I don't grow anything but I have a wife and a son who both have green fingers and love being out there no matter what the weather. They say it is therapeutic, relaxing, creative. That it somehow puts them back in touch with the soil, the earth, nature. I'm just happy to eat the stuff and pour the wine – I know my place – but the vegetable garden does look fantastic, somehow wholesome and incredibly visually satisfying. It's a good dream to make come true.

PROS

It's hugely satisfying to grow and eat your own vegetables.

You know exactly what chemicals and fertilisers have or haven't been used to grow them.

Vegetable gardening is extremely relaxing and therapeutic for those who enjoy it.

A well tended vegetable plot is a thing of beauty.

You feel in touch with the soil and part of a long historic tradition when you grow your own vegetables.

CONS

Unless you're a keen and successful gardener now, you can't assume that moving location will suddenly turn you into one. Vegetable growing is more difficult than you might think.

Growing your own vegetables is very hard work.

Vegetable growing means gluts. The crops won't spread themselves helpfully across the seasons, but all come at once. If you're also a keen cook you can puree, freeze, bottle, pickle and make jam. Otherwise, you'll just have to eat the same thing until you hate the sight of it.

KEY QUESTIONS

II Are you already a keen gardener?

II If not, are you sure you'll turn out to have green fingers? Will you really be happy putting in all those hours in the garden?

II Might you be happier with a lower maintenance garden (that's just about any other kind of garden)?

II Are you fit and healthy enough to cope with heavy duty gardening?

II Are you happy to eat muddy, misshapen vegetables until they're coming out of your ears?

———

=

HAVING A BIG KITCHEN WITH AN AGA

THE DREAM

You pad downstairs in the depths of the winter. It is early morning and you open the kitchen door. The warmth greets you from this big, pine floored, Georgian green, chrome and old hand-written signed vision of country living. You step barefoot across the stripped floor to the Aga. Your loyal and faithful friend awaits you, cats curled around it, kettle waiting to be put on, tea towels drying on the rail, shiny utensils hanging up above it, oven glove purring at you. In the bottom oven a lamb casserole you slipped in the night before bubbles gently, waiting to reach the peak of its home-cooked perfection exactly at lunchtime. This is heaven. This is a big kitchen with an Aga. How did you ever manage in that cramped basement flat in the city with only a Baby Belling for so long?

THE REALITY

I'll tell you how. That old Baby Belling was reliable, easy to clean, affordable, instant and cheap to maintain. Range cookers on the other hand do have some fairly distinct drawbacks. For a start, they take ages to heat up and they take ages to cool down.

You have to turn them off the day before the service engineer arrives or they cannot be worked on. And you have to have them serviced annually which ain't cheap.

You also find that the more you have cooking on a range cooker at the same time the cooler it gets (the heat escapes, you see, as soon as you lift the lid of the hotplate) which means half-raw food or you have to be forward thinking enough to remember to turn them up (several hours ahead of time). Equally, you can't just turn the oven up if the roast potatoes aren't quite ready when the meat is. Or, of course, you can just get into the habit of eating lunch at 4.30 in the afternoon. This irritating little foible of range cookers can be particularly disastrous at times when the cooker gets a lot of use, such as at Christmas.

Most range cookers don't do central heating as well unless you buy an add on boiler. So all that lovely heat you are generating 24 hours a day warms only your kitchen – or at best the kitchen and the hot water. You also have to house and pay for a boiler. Having said that, there are some versions which do run the central heating for you.

Range cookers run on a variety of fuels. They can run on gas, but many houses – including most of those outside villages – don't have access to gas. So it's oil or electricity. Neither of these is cheap (your Aga is on 24 hours a day remember) and if you opt for oil, you'll need a large storage tank and regular visits from the oil supplier. Running out of oil in the middle of winter – and therefore having no heat and no cooker – is one of those little adventures that happen to oil-fired range cooker owners once or twice most winters. Christmas day is the worst for this.

You can get ranges that run on solid fuel, which you have to collect, keep supplied with, chop, lug around or whatever. Unless you're a serious self-sufficiency masochist, my advice is don't go there.

And what happens in the summer? I'll tell you. In the summer they carry on generating all that lovely heat which means your kitchen is far too hot unless it's enormous or you live in

Greenland. You can of course turn off the Aga but then you can't cook on it. And you would then need another electric cooker to cook on. All of which somewhat defeats the object.

Having a big kitchen with an Aga attracts friends. You can't get rid of them. Now, I don't know about you but I'm supposed to be working, not socialising. If you do go out to work then who is getting the benefit of all that lovely heat (which you're paying for) 'cos it certainly ain't you? Friends gather like flies around Agas and can't be budged. And not only friends: passing acquaintances who bore you, neighbours who like eating your food but never invite you back, irritating people who drop in to ask you to do things or get involved in things that you're just not interested in.

Agas are designed to cook wonderful things like drop scones, lamb casseroles, meringues and the like. Have you any idea how an Aga piles the pounds on? No, I thought not or you wouldn't be dreaming of one. And have you ever tried to cook on an Aga? Again, I thought not. You will have to learn a whole new raft of skills. There's no grill you know. You have to trap your toast in a huge metal fishtrap and then sandwich it between the hot plate and the lid and half of it burns and the other half isn't cooked at all. Bit like barbecue food really. Bit like cooking outdoors. You'd better like burnt toast or you'd better buy a toaster. And you can't grill your bacon or your crème brûlées. You can't adjust the oven temperature either, which can be restrictive with a two-oven cooker.

If you have an Aga and a big kitchen you can kiss goodbye to your sitting room because you won't be using it. That may be a good thing because you do get addicted to that warmth in the kitchen. Yes, there is an upside – isn't there always? It is very cosy. It is welcoming. Food does taste better once you've learnt those new culinary skills. What's more, some modern makes of range cooker look old fashioned but heat up from cold in a matter of minutes, and have adjustable oven temperatures.

You can dry out new born lambs in front of an Aga (later you can pop them into the top oven, oh cruel, cruel!). You can dry clothes, shoes, bread tins, whatever. You can bake the best bread in the world in those newly dried tins. You will find kids gather round it, elegant ladies will warm their bums on it, country squires will lean on it and entertain you for hours with lovely country stories and your home will have an ever constant warm heart. Ahhh.

PROS

A range cooker is the heart of the kitchen.

If you're not committed to having an Aga, there are other range cookers with less cachet but more convenience.

Food cooked in a range oven almost never dries out, and consequently tastes fantastic.

Once you've acquired the art of cooking on an Aga, you'll never want to cook on anything else (apart from your bacon, your crème brûlée…).

Your kitchen is constantly warm and inviting.

The cooker doubles as a clothes dryer.

CONS

A range cooker is very expensive (think in thousands). Even the reconditioned ones will set you back a lot more than an ordinary cooker. And beware buying second hand 'buyer collects' — it takes several people to lift an Aga.

An Aga should never be allowed to go out unless you're not planning to use it for days. They take around eight hours to come up to heat. When you lift the lid the heat starts to escape and the oven temperature plummets.

Until you get the hang of it, they're tricky to cook with. There's no grill and you can't adjust the oven temperature.

Solid fuel cookers are a massive hassle and inconvenience, and the romance of keeping them stocked with fuel soon wears off. Oil fired cookers can run out of fuel at the most inconvenient times.

Many ranges, Agas included, won't run the heating.

Your kitchen gets so hot in summer you have to turn the Aga off for two or three months. Which means you need another cooker as well.

Your kitchen is so welcoming that you can't get rid of visitors.

KEY QUESTIONS

II What will a range cooker cost?

II Have you got room for it? How will you flue it?

II Do you really want the cachet of owning an Aga? If not, look at the alternatives. The four oven Aga (if you have the space and the budget for it) is very versatile for cooking. On the other hand, some of the lesser known makes look great (and some look horrible) and have other useful features which make them more flexible to use.

II What will you do about heating the house?

II What kind of fuel supply will you use? What will this cost? How much work will it entail?

II What will you do when the kitchen gets hot in the summer? If you have a second cooker, where will you keep it? What will it cost?

II Are you a keen cook who relishes the prospect of learning a new style of cooking or will you be daunted by it?

＝＝

BEING AWARE OF THE PASSING SEASONS

―――

THE DREAM

You gaze out of your window watching the leaves turn gold and brown and red. They fall and, before you know it, the ground is covered in snow and you are taking brisk walks and coming home to warming log fires, hot chocolate and crumpets and roasting chestnuts. Then it's Christmas and you're celebrating with real Yule logs, and fresh mistletoe picked in your own frosty orchards. And you turn around and it's spring and there are catkins and sticky buds and bursting green and yellow and white, and longer days and warmer evenings and the birds are nesting.

Then it's summer and you watch the swallows return and the kids are playing out on the lawn with a hose pipe 'cos its hotter than hot and you sip Pimms and stay out late eating under the dappled shade of the trees. Just as you start to think about getting in logs for the winter, autumn swings round again as the first mists and mellow fruitfulness ripen and bloom, your vegetable plot is packed with home grown food for harvest time, and the days are getting colder. You feel totally in touch with the seasons because you are so aware of their passing.

THE REALITY

Yes, in the city we haven't a clue what season it is apart from what's in the shops and how cold it is. And even these two indicators can be very deceptive. I've seen Christmas cards in the shops in August and known it cold enough in June for snow.

But once we move to the countryside not knowing will be a thing of the past, right? Well....yes, but being aware of the passing of the seasons might be something you aren't quite so keen on. You see in the city – and big towns – you are protected from nature and the seasons to a great extent. It's all taxis and central heating and warm shops and covered pavements. In the countryside you get it full on, full face, full time, and you might not want it quite so vivid, so raw, so ever present.

In the city you might get your four equal seasons muted and watered down. In the countryside you quickly realise that they aren't equal. Spring and summer and autumn are squashed together into six months of the year (with summer only getting about a month of that and the other two being about two and a half months each). Meanwhile winter is stretched out to last a whole half year – six months of wind and rain and cold and damp. The further north you go the longer the winter lasts.

Look, there's no need at all for anyone to have February – you might as well go to Spain – but in the countryside it is a dominant month and seems to last at least eight weeks. The seasons may seem romantic, evocative, nostalgic, idealistic when you are in the cities and towns but the second you move they become the wrong season. The summer is always too hot and you can't go outside or the kids will burn. The winter is always too cold and you can't go outside or you'll freeze, and the other two seasons are always too damp to go outside in.

The roads are muddy and they flood or freeze. The wind whistles across the open fields and sneaks in under the doors. The rain falls horizontally and makes cars hard to start. God, you're better off in the city not watching the passing of the seasons. The passing of the seasons reminds you of the passing of the years and suddenly you aren't as young as you thought. Time doesn't pass in the city and you can stay young forever; in the country-side the unremitting weather grinds you down faster than any-thing.

That's the bleak view and one a lot of folk in the countryside have. Try telling them you've moved because you want to enjoy the passing of the seasons and they'll think you soft in the head. But it is a dream worth having as long as you are realistic about it. Don't go all gooey eyed and misty talking about nature and the seasons but accept that once you move things are different and you have a living to earn and a house to heat and a car to start and possibly kids to be got to school.

Interference from the weather loses some of its glamour and romance when you're in a hurry or trying to garden or go shopping. But there is still space to be awed by a view or to walk in a bluebell wood in spring and feel so full of wonder you can't speak. There is a rhythm, a tune that you can stay in touch with as long as you stay focused on why you moved in the first place. Don't lose that wonder in the daily round of living.

PROS

There's no doubt that you're aware of the seasons out in the country.

You can smell the beginning of spring or autumn as you step out of your front door.

The variety of surroundings the seasons give you is a delight.

CONS

Winter is by far the longest season in the country, even in the south. Summer is the shortest.

Being more in touch with the seasons means being more in touch with the weather. The bad weather as well as the good.

You can't escape from bad weather into a shopping mall or a coffee shop or an underground station. Everything you do, from filling the car up with petrol to dropping the kids at school is done in the face of whatever the seasons can throw at you: gale, blizzard or drenching rain.

If you've organised your country dream to include chopping logs for the fire, growing your own vegetables, keeping a horse or any other wonderful, rural activities, you'll be more aware of your outdoor surroundings than you might choose.

KEY QUESTIONS

II The passing seasons bring beautiful views and smells. They also bring varied weather. How long is the winter in the part of the country you're looking to move into? What is the average rainfall (some places are much wetter than others)? Is it particularly windy?

II When you find a house you want to buy, what shelter will it give you in winter? Does the house face the wildest weather or is it nestled in a snug valley? Does it have porches, outhouses and garages to hide from the worst of the rain and gales in? Or will you be exposed to blustering storms every time you nip out to the car or go to feed the chickens? How close to the door can you park?

II How well do you cope with being wet and cold? Don't kid yourself you'll feel differently once you're a country dweller. Except in the sense that you'll feel wetter and colder than you ever thought possible back in the city.

GETTING BACK TO NATURE

THE DREAM

You slip out of the house just as light is beginning to show in the east. The air is still and cold and you have your thickest coat on to ward off the chill of the dawn air. You walk through the woods listening as the crunch of leaves is soft beneath your laced boots. You pause for a moment as you spot a deer slipping through the trees. In the trees above your head squirrels are beginning to chatter and quarrel over food; a fox slinks across the path ahead and you catch sight of a badger making its late way home.

All is still and quiet and you experience a complete sense of belonging, of coming home, of being at one with everything growing and living.

THE REALITY

Indeed a lot of us townies do dream of being at one with nature. We dream of camping out in the wilds, of walking the hills, of riding horses across the edge of the sea on some deserted beach. Sometimes we dream of being more than mere observer; perhaps the hunter, the angler, the trapper, the poacher. We dream of catching our own wild food and cooking it on small fires deep in

the woods, or by the river bank, using the best Hugh Fearnley-Eatitall recipes, or on the beach frying up freshly caught fish like Rick himself.

Perhaps we imagine watching birds, capturing in our notebook the rare and the unusual. We dream of being full time twitchers. Perhaps we fantasise about being wise country folk knowing what herbs heal and cure, what to cook with from the hedgerows, what mushrooms to use and what toadstools to leave. Within a month of moving to the countryside we'll be using spider's web to cure headaches, getting rid of warts with the merest rub of a freshly cut hawthorn twig. We imagine ourselves cooking nettle soup, gathering sloes to make our own gin, harvesting the brambles to make pies and storing the surplus cob nuts in our own sheds.

All say 'ahhh'. All say 'in your dreams'. Listen, this ain't gonna happen. Oh, it might for a few successful ones who've done their research but for the rest of us townies we are going to be terribly, bitterly disappointed. Almost the only folk in the country who know all this stuff are townies with decent text books. The country folk are trying as hard as possible to get away from nature. Why? Because it is cold and damp, unfriendly, dangerous, red in tooth and claw, smelly and thin on the ground. I once stood in a logging yard buying wood for the fire, and watched a beautiful kestrel hovering overhead. The log man glanced up to see what I was looking at. "Ar" he said. "It's a 'awk."

Getting back to nature is fine in books or on TV but the reality is colder, wetter, harsher, funnier. You try sleeping out under the stars and you'll discover how wet it is in the mornings. You try fishing and you'll get done for poaching. You try riding horses across deserted beaches and they'll have the law on you. You try eating from the hedgerows and you'll poison yourself. You try cooking on a beach and you'll find out how windy it is, how easy it is to forget the matches or the firelighters or the wood or the plates or the fish. You try walking in the woods at dawn and you'll see how little you'll see and exactly how cold it is.

Cynical? No, not a bit. Just trying to make sure you approach these things realistically, honestly, open mindedly and with goals that are achievable. If you set your sights too high you'll be bound for disappointment but if you set them realistically and are prepared in advance for adventures, laughs and whatever comes then you'll get on just fine in the countryside. When it works it's fantastic. You'll enjoy those early morning walks, the hunting/shooting/fishing (if that's your bag), the camping, the nature rambles, the outdoor cooking, the wild food from the hedgerows.

Before you throw it all in and move to the countryside take a moment to consider exactly what you mean by 'being part of nature'. It's an easy phrase to use but what exactly do you mean by it? Also remember that the countryside is evocative, beautiful, haunting, when we live in the city. Once we have moved it becomes everyday, normal, and we grow complacent about it and start to take it for granted. To keep it fresh we have to appreciate it anew everyday, take time out to look at it simply and with the eyes of a child (yuck) and then we'll find we are part of nature unconsciously, naturally (pass the sick bag, someone).

PROS

The best nature moments in the countryside may be rarer than you imagine but, when they happen, they are wonderful.

Just driving to work past fields rather than tower blocks has to be an improvement on living in the city.

CONS

In your imagination, getting back to nature gives you a warm feeling. In reality, it more often gives you a cold feeling. And a damp, uncomfortable one.

A lot of your local nature actually belongs to someone else. You're not necessarily allowed to walk in those woods, or camp in that field, or ride your horse across those dunes.

You need to be prepared for a fair amount of ridicule while you learn how to get the most of getting back to nature.

All your dreamed-of natural pursuits take time. If you have a living to earn or a family to run it may not be easy finding time to go badger watching or fungus finding.

KEY QUESTIONS

II What exactly do you mean by getting back to nature? What activities do you want to try?

II How much time is your new lifestyle going to allow for these sorts of activities?

II How feasible will it be in the area you're looking at moving into? Do they have badgers/access to fungus woods/ suitable rivers and so on?

II How hardy are you? Much as you might like to fool yourself, you're not going to change personality just because you change locality. If you hate being wet, cold and uncomfortable you're not suddenly going to start enjoying it. Would you really enjoy getting back to nature if you had the chance?

HAVING OPEN FIRES AND WOOD BURNERS

THE DREAM

You lazily stretch out your legs and warm those weary toes by the dying embers of your fire. Time for bed. The room is warm and you get up and put another couple of logs on the fire, safe in the knowledge that in the morning all it will take is a couple of puffs with the bellows to get it roaring again.

And in the morning it is the red embers that spring into life and provide you with instant heat. Outside a gale is blowing but in here it is snug and warm and cosy. Ah, there's nothing like an open fire or a wood burner. Think chestnuts, Yule logs, toast on forks, marshmallows, socks and gloves drying, the kettle whistling, fairies in the flames and the smell of smoke and oak burning.

THE REALITY

It's a good fantasy. It is easily attainable and provides instant evocative country living. You don't have open fires in the town – smoke regulations probably stop you even if the fireplaces haven't been boarded over or bricked up long ago. Here in the

country you can live out your dream with your back to the fire as you warm your buttocks, glass of wine in hand and regale your guests with lovely tales of 'when we lived in the city in the old days blah blah'. Lovely. OK but – it's only a tiny but – but there are a couple of things you ought to be aware of before committing to this dream.

Firstly, the reason they had open fires in the olden days was because that was all that was available. They put up with the drawbacks because there was no alternative. Now there is and I'm afraid we might have grown a little used to the alternatives – central heating, electric fires, gas fires, oil radiators, under floor heating, convectors, hot air, Calor gas – you name it. And the thing they all provide is instant heat. Get it? Instant. Now the one thing an open fire doesn't provide is anything instant. As a background it's fine. As a device for providing atmosphere, brilliant. But as for providing instant heat, forget it. You try coming in from work freezing, chilled to the bone, soaked from all that winter rain and you'll see what I mean.

First you've got to bring in the wood/coal/whatever. Then you're on your knees laying it – paper or firelighters – with stiff cold fingers. Then there's the lighting and then there's the waiting. Eventually there are flames and very limited heat. After quite a time (by when you've keeled over with hypothermia) you get your heat. Sometimes too much. You try turning down an open fire or shutting down a wood burner and you realise just exactly what the opposite of instant is.

Wood burning stoves take a long time to give off heat and you don't get quite the same romantic open flame thing you get with an old fashioned fire. On the other hand, all that metal radiates heat and warms the room once it gets going. With an open fire, about eighty percent of the heat goes straight up the chimney. Unless you have a tiny, low-ceilinged room or an immense fireplace, it won't be enough to heat the room in winter.

Both fires and stoves can takes months or even years to get right. By that I mean that they often smoke, and even a skilled chimney sweep can't always tell you why. You would think that in an old property, a fireplace that has been used for maybe hundreds of years would have been sorted out by now. Often they have, but many of them still smoke appallingly. Since fires are dangerous you really need a smoke alarm, and this will go off whenever the fire smokes.

Even a reliable fire will usually start smoking if you fiddle with the fireplace, the flue, the chimney or the cowl, or replace the firebasket, or add a woodburner, or change the woodburner... yes, it can be hard work getting your fire to stop spewing smoke into the room. Many fires go well if the wind is in one direction but not another, or require the door to the room to be shut, or only stop smoking if you push the fire basket right to the back so *all* the heat goes up the chimney.

Open fires basically are messy, dirty, smelly (you do get rooms full of smoke when the wind is in the wrong direction), time consuming (you get to carry ashes out and fuel in, a lot), hard work and dangerous. They spit sparks, start chimney fires, throw out burning logs when you're out of the room and burn children when you're not looking.

The biggest drawback with them is updraught. What? Updraught. As they burn they send lots of lovely warm air, hot air, up the chimney. That air has to be replaced or you'll die of suffocation. So draughts sneak in. Wind howls in under the doors, through the gaps around the windows. Yes, your toes might be warming but your back will freeze. Get a life, get central heating. No? Then enjoy your fire or wood burner but be realistic about it.

We lived here in our draughty old farmhouse for the first five years with no heating except an open fire. It was romantic, cold, evocative, dreamy. In the depths of the winter we scuttled from room to room fast. We wore lots of jumpers. We roasted chestnuts and did all that stuff and it was great. And cold. When the chil-

dren came along we installed central heating. Brilliant. Warm. Easy. But we have kept the open fires and the wood burner. In the evenings they are still the best thing to sit in front of and toast our toes. We wouldn't be without them, but it's tough relying on them as your only heating.

Another frequent disadvantage of anything with a chimney is that while *you're* trying to get the smoke to go up it, all sorts of other things are trying to get down it. Birds appear every so often in your living room. If you're out for a while they'll have crapped all over your furniture before you get home. Bird nests get stuck in the chimney in late spring and wreak havoc the next time you light the fire in the autumn.

Oh and one last drawback. Hormones. You cannot have a male visitor without they feel the need to poke your fire. Women don't seem to do this but men always want to. Why? Is it a cave thing? It drives me mad and they seem to put out more fires than they encourage or help. It's a boy thing. Take my advice and never leave male visitors or children alone with your fires.

Apart from that and the dirt and work and the draughts and the constant supply of logs they consume which ain't cheap (and someone has to chop them or have them delivered and you have to stack them and then carry them in) and the slowness to warm you up and the ash and the having to have your chimneys swept twice a year – they're brilliant. They have visual appeal but don't rely on them for your heat.

PROS

There are few things more romantic and cosy than a real fire.

The right fire, once it gets going, can give off a decent amount of heat.

You can warm your toes, roast chestnuts or dry out your gloves better on an open fire than almost anything else.

CONS

It takes a long time for a real fire to give off any heat.

It may never give off enough heat to warm the room.

Many fires and stoves smoke worse than you can stand, and it can take ages to resolve the problem.

Fires are messy and dirty, making rooms dusty and sooty and harder to clean.

Fires actually cause draughts, sucking in air to replace the oxygen they burn.

It's hard work having an open fire. Chopping logs seems deeply romantic from the comfort of a city home, but in reality the novelty wears off pretty fast. Even if you have them delivered ready chopped, you almost certainly still have to stack them, and carry them into the house.

It takes a few minutes to make a fire. By the time you've fetched the logs, and laid and lit the fire, that's several minutes work. That may not sound like much, but every day, when you're trying to get a meal ready, or unpack the shopping, or sort the kids out, it soon gets irritating.

Real fires are dangerous. You can't leave small children alone in the room with a fire, and even a wood burning stove needs to be well protected. Spitting logs and sparks can start house fires, and trying to burn cardboard or paper on a fire can cause chimney fires (trust me, I've been there).

KEY QUESTIONS

II Do you want real fires to provide all the warmth in the house, or will you use some other form of heating?

II Do you prefer open fires or wood burning stoves? Stoves will give you more heat, but fires are more traditionally romantic. You could consider a stove with large doors you can keep open as a compromise.

II If you want to use fires alone, at least in some rooms, how will you cope with being cold a lot of the time?

II If you have children, how will you keep them safe near the fire?

II Are you picky about having a clean house? Fires create a lot more dirt and mess.

II Do you enjoy the challenge of sorting out fires that smoke or don't give enough heat, or will you just become impatient and fed up? If you hate this kind of thing, you might be better off not relying on the fire for heat. That way you can just abandon it for a few weeks if it's driving you mad, and wait until you can face dealing with it again.

II How much do you enjoy hard work? The times you need logs are when you need fires – that's the cold, windy, wet days. How will you feel about chopping and fetching in logs in a howling gale, day after day? If you don't like this kind of work (and I wouldn't blame you), at least try to plan fireplaces where you can store several days' worth of logs at once.

———

SENDING THE KIDS TO A BETTER SCHOOL

THE DREAM

Your delightful children toddle off to school with their satchels neatly ironed and their lunchboxes full of wholesome ploughman's cheese and bread and an apple plucked from your own trees. The school is within walking distance and the classes small, the teachers dedicated and brilliant, the curriculum varied and interesting and the out-of-school clubs stimulating and challenging.

Your children thrive and do well and go on to a country university where they excel and graduate with honours, having had the benefit of such inspiring schooling.

THE REALITY

We can all imagine the scene where our children follow the track past the cornfields to the village school where they get the best education possible. Unfortunately it isn't always quite like that. It may be in the movies, but real life can be somewhat different. For a start village schools are closing at such a rate that they may all be gone before you even get there. If you are lucky to find

one still open and fully functioning you may not be able to get your child in – they can be horribly over-subscribed.

Once you do get your children in forget all ideas of them walking to school unless it's within a few hundred yards:

II They won't walk – they'll moan it's too far (and they may well be right) and none of their classmates walk.

II Coming from the city you'll worry about molesters, muggers, kidnappers.

II It rains more than you think in the country and the lanes get very muddy and impassable.

II Country lanes can be downright dangerous for walking especially in the early mornings or on dark winter evenings – no street lights remember.

II School buses may be over subscribed or not be available at all.

Once at school they may not get quite the education you expect. Country schools are used to churning out country folk – they get the education they are likely to need and without being too pessimistic they may well be educated to farm or factory level if that is all they are likely to need. I once lived in a country town where 75 percent of all pupils left school to go to work in the two main industries in the town – brewing and shoe making. The other 25 percent? Oh, about 10 percent had to travel 15 miles to go to a sixth-form college, and they were the lucky ones. The unlucky ones – the remaining 15 percent – left to go straight on the dole.

Assuming you find a good school and are happy with the journey you may be surprised to find the level of teaching not quite what you expect. Yes, it may be on a par with the very best city schools; on the other hand it may be second rate and less than perfect. If the level of wages is lower in the country the better teachers may have already left for the city to chase the money – doing your journey in reverse. Village schools are generally small and often teach several year groups in the same class. Your child may not even have classmates their own age at the school. You may be reduced to sending your child to a private school (and thus making them and you stand out as townies). However, you may find that the only decent private schools around are so far away they have to board.

After school clubs? You'll be lucky. You might get the occasional school disco but you are just as likely to get nothing at all. City folk have a greater level of expectation for their children where country folk see schooling as something to get the kids out of the house during the day. These are, of course, sweeping generalisations. You have to do your research in advance. You may find good schools with good teachers and small classes close to your new country home but don't wait until you've moved before finding out. Your children are going to have a hard enough job making new friends and fitting in without having to travel vast distances with all that entails.

PROS

If you can find a good local school the class sizes may be smaller than in many city schools.

Small schools in small communities feel safe because the parents and children all know each other and look out for each other.

An underconfident child — or a child coping with the upheaval of being downshifted by its parents — may feel more secure in a smaller, local school.

Children often thrive socially in small schools.

CONS

You'll end up doing the school run even in the depths of the winter when the roads haven't been gritted and the mud is thick and skiddy.

The school may not give you the level of education you have come to expect.

The class sizes can be large and the teaching less than perfect.

Your children may struggle to get suitable qualifications.

KEY QUESTIONS

II How close are the local schools?

II What sort of public transport is there?

II How heavily subscribed are the schools?

II Is there a sixth form?

II Where do their school leavers go on to?

II Is the school in any danger of closing?

II What is the average class size?

II What extra-curricular activities/clubs are there?

———

Keeping chickens

THE DREAM

The cockerel crows to wake you just after dawn. The sun is up and so must you be. This is far too nice a day to stay in bed. You put on a pot of coffee and some rashers of bacon and go in search of the eggs. You open the back door and, carrying your little wicker basket, wander off to the hen house. You release the hens, who cluck contentedly around your feet. You throw them a couple of handfuls of corn which you scatter on the grass for them to peck for. You open up the back of the hen house and find four beautiful brown eggs nestling in the little nest of hay. Perfect. Two eggs each for you and your partner.

You leave the hens to their happy pecking and are back in the house just as the coffee begins to boil and the bacon to crisp up. Breaking the eggs into the frying pan you see delicious golden yolks and life couldn't be richer.

THE REALITY

It isn't usually quite like that. If it is you will be amazingly lucky. The reality is a little less rose-tinted. But as townies what do we know about keeping chickens anyway? I did have a friend who said she couldn't keep chickens because it meant having so

many. When asked what she meant she explained that you had to have one cockerel to every hen. Oh, how we laughed, but why shouldn't she have believed that, she was a townie. (By the way you only need one cockerel to as many hens as he is physically capable of servicing – if you want live chicks – and the answer to how many is that, is a lot more than you would think).

Let's have a quick look at this dream which so many of us have, which so many of us move to the country in search of. To begin with, you're going to need somewhere to house your chickens. Maybe you can convert an old shed or you will have to buy a pur-pose built wooden hen house which costs from about £75, for a house for 2 hens, up to several hundred pounds. It will take you a long time to recoup the money saved on egg buying. Letting the chickens out means they will:

II Scratch up all your flower beds.

II Eat all your garden produce unless you fence it off or fence the chickens out.

II Shit all over your garden furniture.

II Escape so they can get eaten by the predators – see below.

II A cockerel is liable to attack small children – and they do crow at all hours of the night and your nearest neighbours will complain even if they live half a mile away.

II Keeping them in a run means they will turn any plot of land into a barren dust bowl capable of growing only nettles. And they'll need letting in and out every night and morning, fenc-ing off or in, regular feeding which means buying corn or chicken pellets (if you feed them household scraps you'll attract the rats – see below).

Throwing handfuls of food around isn't hygienic. It attracts rats, squirrels and other pests. The squirrels have to be trapped and moved at least 2 miles away or they'll chew up your hen house. They love to gnaw. Even if you leave the door open they will gnaw their way in. They are singularly stupid animals, even as stupid as chickens and they really are stupid. Rats, I'm afraid, have to be poisoned or shot or killed by a small vicious dog which you will have to hire or borrow – no, you don't want to own one. If you don't kill the rats they will steal the eggs (as will the squirrels, magpies, jackdaws and jays), kill the chicks (and not necessarily eat them) and spread diseases.

Chickens really are stupid animals. They love to escape so they can throw themselves into the arms of the nearest fox. If the fox gets into the hen house – and they will do the one night you forget to shut your chickens in – they'll play the 'kill me first' game with singular success. If your chickens do get out they'll not have the intelligence to roost in the trees but will instead curl up happily in the undergrowth where any passing fox or badger will have them as a tasty snack. It has been known for harriers, buzzards and falcons to take chickens. Mink will also take them. Keeping chickens can be a tooth and claw business.

If your chickens do lay eggs – and they may not as 'broodiness' is a full time occupation for lots of them (especially the rare breeds, hence their rarity) – you can't assume you will get them before anyone or anything else has them, and before your bacon has crisped up nicely. For a start the rats will take them as we saw earlier, along with many other predators such as the squirrels and jays. You may even find you have an egg-eating chicken – not as rare as you might think.

Chickens lay far less in the winter than the summer, and many breeds stop laying all together between October and February unless you provide them with electric light to con them into thinking the days are longer than they are.

Technically, even if you keep chickens only as a hobby or as pets, you have to inform the relevant authorities if any die (they are classified as farm animals and subject to all the usual regulations re foot and mouth, animal transportation etc) and you have to pay the local knacker's yard for the carcasses to be removed to be incinerated. You are allowed to eat them but not to feed them to your dog/s. You are not allowed to bury them. It's all more hassle.

But keeping chickens can also be extremely rewarding just so long as you approach it with your eyes opened. For a start, it makes you get out twice a day, however busy you are, to let them out/shut them in, which gives you a breath of fresh air and gets you away from your computer. And of course, if you are success-ful – or is that lucky? – you get lots of lovely fresh eggs.

You get to choose what your hens eat and what sort of lifestyle they'll have so your eggs will be healthier and you'll be con-tributing something useful to the environment, and you can get into keeping rare breed chickens which is very entertaining. If you keep a cockerel and manage to keep your neighbours happy you can breed your own chicks which is fun and has a tremen-dous 'ahh' factor, and the kids will love it.

If you manage to beat the rats and the fox, stop your chickens getting out and committing suicide, can afford the cost of hen houses and remember to let them out you may indeed find the dream of fresh eggs for breakfast a distinct possibility.

PROS

When things go right, you get plenty of fresh eggs, at least during the spring and summer. And you know what went into them so you can make them as organic and healthy as you please.

It gets you out of the house twice a day.

If you've always dreamed of keeping hens, you get a buzz out of the sight of them happily clucking around.

Believe it or not you can form a sort of relationship with your chickens and they make good pets.

They provide an easy educational experience for children about animal husbandry.

CONS

Chicken keeping can be hard work. Although your daily chores may take only a few minutes, there are bouts of very hard work getting the better of vermin and predators.

Hen houses are either hard work to build or expensive to buy.

You can't assume that eggs will simply happen. You may go months without seeing any.

Chickens are messy and smelly, and cockerels are downright noisy. This can make you unpopular with your neighbours.

Hens tie you down. Someone has to let them out every morning and shut them in every evening. And if you want to go on holiday you have to find someone to look after them morning and evening.

Chicken keeping can be heartbreaking (you do actually cry when a fox has killed all your hens and it hasn't even eaten any of them).

KEY QUESTIONS

II How many hens do I want? (Each will give you, very approximately, two eggs per three days in season.)

II Where will I keep them?

II Will my hens be free range or are they to be kept in a run?

II What will a suitable hen house cost?

II How much will it cost to feed them?

II Do I need a cockerel? What will my neighbours say if I do keep a cockerel?

II What do I do with the surplus eggs if I get any?

II What do I do with the surplus chicks if I get them?

II What do I do with the surplus chicken manure which I will definitely get?

=

KEEPING A HORSE

THE DREAM

A shy whinnying comes from the paddock and you look out of the kitchen window. There, cantering across the grass, kicking up his heels is the love of your life. The horse. He is proud and brown and shiny and handsome. And he is yours, all yours. Later, after coffee, you will go out and saddle him and take him out across the moors, riding him proudly as he holds his head high. You have this perfect bond, you and him. He knows what you want and how to walk and gallop and trot when you want him to. His stable, which you had built, smells of his warmth. This feels like home to you now. This is what you moved to the country for. This is equestrian heaven. You and your proud animal moving together in perfect harmony of horse and rider.

THE REALITY

Well, it don't come cheap. And it don't come without a lot of hard work either. And it don't come without a lot of heartache and a lot of soul searching. Look, before you ever embark on this madness – dangerous at both ends and uncomfortable in the middle – you have to be pretty sure you know exactly what you want. What sort of a horse are you going to go for? What do you want it for? Dressage? Jumping? Showing? Pony club? Hacking? Riding round the lanes driving us motorists bananas? How big? How old?

I didn't realise there were so many horses and types of horses and reasons for having a horse until I started researching this particular dream. (Not one of mine I must admit.) My local horse feed shop – plug here for Red Post Equestrian – says you should think of a horse in the same way you think of a car. There's your Rolls Royce and your 4x4, your 2CV and your Transit van. Each costs a certain amount and each does a job and each appeals to a particular type and each causes its own problems. Hey, its your dream and you ought to know a lot about horses before you try to make this one come true. Right?

You are going to need an awful lot of stuff before you even get round to buying the horse. There's stabling, tack, feeding, hay, rugs, brushes and mucking out stuff. It's a long list and none of it is cheap. Average prices for the kit alone are from five hundred quid to well over five thousand. A saddle on its own can cost the best part of a grand.

Stabling. Now that's a good one. Got one of your own? Fine and good but if you haven't you'll need to buy one – another few grand – and get planning permission to have it installed. And you'll need running water and probably electricity. If you don't have one of your own you can go DIY and rent stabling. Average cost is around £20 a box. That's twenty quid a week, every week, rain or shine. Plus another twenty quid a week for food. See, I said it was expensive. And then there's the cost of hay. And driving to the stable twice a day, every day. That eats into your time and holidays and weekends.

Hey, you wanna talk about vet's bills yet? No? Well, considering they charge £30-40 a call out and that's without the cost of drugs or medication or equipment and you're probably right not to want to talk about it. The horse's teeth alone can cost you a fortune. And the blacksmith? Again they ain't cheap – about £45 a visit – and you'll need them to come every six weeks (it should really be once a month but no one can afford that). OK, let's gloss over the cost of stabling and vets and blacksmiths and the tie and the time and the mounting feed bills. Let's instead talk about insurance. No? What about security? Theft of horses goes on you know. Look, it's no good not listening and putting your fingers in your ears. You are going to have to take this stuff into account if you are to realise your dream. We're not saying 'no', we're merely saying look at it carefully before committing.

Oh yes, we forgot the cost of the horse itself. Now there's a piece of string for you. Sure, you can pick up a Dartmoor pony for thirty quid but it might not be what you want. So how much? Anything from a hundred pounds for a knackered old pensioned off hacker to half a million for a decent breeding stud. Somewhere in between? Sure, pick a figure and double it and then double it again.

Our local horse feed shop says 'whatever a townie buys first time will always without exception be totally unsuitable'. There, now you've heard it from the horse's mouth. Red Post Equestrian say you can expect to pay around three thousand for something half decent, half worth having. Personally, I'd have thought you'd be better off buying a decent Landrover for half that but then I'm biased.

From what I hear and see having a horse is an enormous financial and emotional burden. But one that those who are doing it wouldn't shirk from. They love it. They love the mucking out and the being tied and the responsibility. They love the arguments with motorists – both sides think they own the road – and the being out in all weathers and the never going away on holiday because they can't get anyone to look after their horses and the vet's bills and the going lame and the worming and the shoeing and the clothing you have to buy, and the hay bills and the equine dysautonomia[1] and the curbs and snaffles[2] and the saddle sores and the falling off and the Recurrent Airway Obstruction (RAO)[3].

They really do seem happy. They had a dream and they have achieved it and in doing so have also realised a deep and meaningful bonding that they talk of in almost mystical terms – rider and horse, animal and human. For them it has been worth it a hundred times over. I guess for them it was a one horse race.

Last thing. If you are thinking of getting a horse to save on grass cutting, forget it. They don't eat dock or nettles or thistles. You'd be better off with a donkey.

PROS

If you enjoy riding, there's nothing like having your own horse.

The relationship between a horse and its owner is unlike any other.

You really know you're in the country when you're riding a horse along the green lanes and down tracks where cars don't go.

You get a great view from horseback, over the hedges that you can't see past in a car.

CONS

The cost has to be the biggest single drawback. Before you consider stabling, you're looking at several thousand pounds just to get set up with a horse and all the gubbins that goes with it. And the running costs aren't much better. What's more, a horse starts depreciating pretty early on, so you can't make your money back on it.

You need a minimum of two acres of land per horse.

You're very tied with a horse. What are you going to do with it when you go on holiday? Or just away for the weekend? Or when you've caught a bug and are too ill to get out of bed?

---

[1] Grass sickness – well you'd be sick of eating grass all the time, wouldn't you?

[2] Bits of the bit, so to speak

[3] Horse cough – a hacking cough?

It's hard work keeping a horse. All that mucking out and lugging feed bags and tack around. It's not for the faint-hearted. And you have to do it in freezing rain in winter, as well as on balmy summer mornings.

Horses occupy your mind and can be a worry. From how you'll pay for them to whether there's dangerous ragwort in the hay, or where you'll find the time to exercise them, they are an ever-present concern.

Traffic can be a problem if you have nowhere to exercise your horse off-road. It's dangerous at the best of times, and even more so if your horse is at all skittish or highly-strung.

KEY QUESTIONS

II What do you want a horse for?

II Where will you keep it? Do you need enough land to keep it yourself, or will you use a livery stables? If you plan to keep it on your own land, what will building stables cost? Will you get planning permission?

II Where will you exercise it? And when will you find the time?

II How will you pay for it? How will you pay for the ongoing costs?

II Who will look after the horse when you're not there? Or will you never go away? It's not like finding someone to feed the cat, after all; you need someone experienced to look after your horse.

II Are you fit enough to cope with all the hard work? And will you enjoy it or come to resent it – especially in the worst weather?

Doing up an old barn

THE DREAM

All the charm of an old country building but with mod cons – you get to choose exactly where and how everything is. You get vast spaces, beams, the satisfaction of getting something new from something that has become redundant. Good views, surrounded by lush countryside. What more could you want? This is your dream. You anticipate the day when you can move in and begin to live in the good space. Here you can breathe. Here you can have a dog, fab Sunday lunches, lots of guests coming to stay, wonderfully warm winter evenings roasting your chestnuts in front of a roaring log fire.

THE REALITY

Marvellous. Main trouble is that these days, not many people are able to make this one come true. How come? A mix of more restrictive planning regulations and the fact that we've already done up almost as many barns as were ever built. Each year there will be fewer and fewer, and they will be increasingly expensive. However, it's not only barns. There are mills, churches and chapels, the occasional lighthouse, and other country buildings you may be able to find ready for conversion.

So if you are one of the lucky ones what can you realistically expect? We'll talk about what you'll end up with in a moment but the actual conversion process may be more troublesome than you'd think. For a start you have to find your barn (or whatever), negotiate for it – and there will be a lot of competition – get your planning permission, find your architect (no, don't think of doing it yourself unless you are either an architect yourself or completely mad), find your local builders and then lastly settle back to living in a caravan in a sea of mud for several times as long as anyone said you would. Still interested? Good.

Let's have a look at what you are actually converting. Suppose you have found an old barn. Where and what? Firstly most, if not all, barns are on farms. Yep, those old smelly, noisy places. That's what you get. And as for what, well basically a building that used to house animals. This means few if any windows, unheated vast spaces, possibly no decent foundations, that sort of thing. Your basic shell may take an awful lot just to get it ready to do up.

Maybe you've found a mill – inevitably near water, so dangerous for kids and prone to flooding. Or a church – draughty with high ceilings (for which read 'impossible to heat') and quite possibly overlooking a graveyard. Or a lighthouse or windmill – exposed to the weather, windswept and with all those stairs.

We won't dwell on the actual doing up process with all the heartache and disappointment that it entails – you will have watched those TV programmes on Channel 4 – but you will have to learn to enjoy the process or it won't be worth it. The dream is *doing up* an old barn, not necessarily living in an old barn or even owning an old barn. But the doing up process is at best only around a year in that old barn's life. You do have to keep the end product in mind – a new old barn.

And what do you get? Vast spaces? Yes, sure. Vast spaces that cost a fortune to heat and have to be furnished. This means big furniture which is more expensive than small stuff. Here I may be teaching my grandmother – that's you that is – to suck eggs and other country pursuits. You know all this stuff. You've weighed up the pros and cons and decided you really can't live anywhere except in an old barn. Good for you.

I've known people buy barns to do up and then not be able to get permission to convert them. I've known 'em run out of money before the project was completed. In one case the couple simply moved their caravan inside the barn and carried on living in it there until they had earned enough money to finish the job. I've known people finish the job and then find they didn't like living in such a big place as they felt overwhelmed by it.

Of course all this goes for chapels, boat houses, churches, bake-houses, dairies, mills, factories, schools and anything else that you want to convert from its original function.

But whatever you convert, you do end up with an unusual living space and one that you designed yourself. You get to have every-thing where you wanted it and how you wanted it – assuming you can afford it. You have the satisfaction of having restored an old building, given it a new lease of life. You've got to employ local people which usually means you get to know everyone and settle into a local community much quicker. And you've got all the attraction and charm of an old building but with modern amenities such as plumbing and under-floor heating.

As long as you allow for the fact that it will take far longer, cost three times as much, and you'll end up living near a working farm which starts as early as six in the morning and you'll be forever surrounded by mud and animals, then you'll do just fine.

PROS

A conversion gives you exactly the living space you want.

You'll end up with an unusual and interesting property.

You get the atmosphere and history of an old house, but with all mod cons.

You can often congratulate yourself on saving a property that might otherwise have decayed beyond repair.

CONS

Properties for conversion are extremely hard to find these days, especially barns.

This means that they are expensive — and that's before you've even started work.

The conversion process will take far longer than you expect — no matter what it is that you expect.

Ditto cost.

Barns are sited on smelly, noisy farms. Mills are always damp and close to water. Many types of building you might be thinking of converting have inherent disadvantages you simply can't get away from.

Coping with builders is unbelievably stressful. If you think getting a plumber round to fix a leaky tap is a hassle, you could end up with a coronary before the builders have even unloaded their van.

Converted spaces are almost always large. Presumably that's part of why you wanted a conversion. But this also means they need big furniture to fill them, they will be extremely expensive to heat, and — if you opt for open-plan living — there won't be much privacy between the main rooms. It's a great style of living, but it's not for everyone.

KEY QUESTIONS

II Why do you want to convert? Is it the process? The personalised design? The kind of space you get at the end of it? Would you actually be happier with a property that has already been converted (plenty of those around)?

II What kind of building do you want to convert? Does it have to be a barn? What about a school, a mill, a church?

II What are the inherent drawbacks of whatever type of building you fancy? Barns are always on farms, mills are by water, churches and even chapels are in villages or towns and not right off the beaten track. Think through what you can expect of the kind of building you think you want.

⁍ How much can you afford to spend? And what could you stretch to if costs escalate as the work continues (which they will)? Look for a low enough purchase cost and building quotes that you have plenty of funds in hand. Conversion costs can easily double as the work goes on.

⁍ What will you do while you're converting the property? Can you afford to keep on your existing property? If so, how far away is it, and will you be able to visit frequently enough to keep a close eye on the building work? If you can't afford it, will you rent? Or live on site? How long can you stand living in a cramped caravan? Assume the conversion will take at least half as long again as you've been quoted. And get time penalty clauses written into the contract.

⁍ What are you like with stress? Can your lifestyle cope with the overwhelming stress of having the builders in for several months at least? This may influence how nearby you want to be. Arm's length is less stressful day to day, but harder to keep the pressure on the builders. Even with penalty clauses built in to the contract (which is advisable) the builders still need plenty of 'encouragement' to complete the job on schedule.

⁍ Do you enjoy living in large spaces? Have you tried it? How do you feel about open-plan? Think through these issues before you finalise your plans for the conversion.

⁍ Have you considered buying a conversion already in development, so you can have a say in the conversion? You can often influence the layout and such things as fixtures and fittings if you do this.

=

A CREATIVE PLACE TO WRITE OR PAINT

THE DREAM

A purpose built log cabin overlooking a stream. Power is laid on for your laptop and there is only peace and quiet. In such tranquillity you produce unbelievably wonderful work that you can instantly sell to fund such a relaxing and worthwhile lifestyle. In the corner you have a little wood burning stove to keep you warm in the winter and hot coffee on tap. You find the atmosphere stimulating and creative. You think green thoughts and are undisturbed and left to work at your own pace. God, it sounds so great I think I'll have a go myself. Hang on, I do already.

THE REALITY

Working from home in the depths of the country can be a little different. For a start you might not be able to get planning permission for the log cabin in the garden and building regs won't allow it anyway so close to a water course.

The biggest problem you'll find with being creative in the countryside is that most of your work has to be done indoors. The screen of your laptop reflects the sunshine in the garden, or it's

raining and you need to be indoors to stay dry. Consequently you'll find you are indoors pretty well no matter what the weather or you're outdoors feeling guilty because you're not working. I guess that unless you are actually painting most creative work has to be done indoors – pottery, printing, photographic dark-room development, sculpting, writing.

And if you do manage to stay indoors to do some work then you'll find the day is taken up with lots of peripheral things that eat time. There is a huge array of distractions, diversions and displacement activities. Let me elaborate.

For a start, if you have kids, there's the school run. You can't pop the little darlings on a bus – there aren't any round here. They can't walk; too far and too dangerous. The school run is moderately fine in summer except you do have a problem rounding them up and getting them into the car – sometimes you have a major problem finding them as they tend to escape into the garden and hide in the undergrowth (yes, there is more of this than there is neat garden. You could do more gardening but then you'd get less work done…). In winter you'll be beset with mud, floods, cattle crossing the roads, more mud, fog, darkness and incredibly slow tractors.

Then there are the friends who assume that because you are at home it's fine to drop in for coffee. There's a lot of them. You may not know anyone when you first move, but you'll be amazed how quickly you meet people who want to drop in for coffee in the daytime. Some of them are quite nice so you'll want to stop and chat.

Then there's the post. Psychologically most of us can't start work until the post has been. Some weeks that's fine. Others not so good. You see, where we are in Devon we have two postmen (yep, men) and one is called Worm and one is called Grub. Now Worm arrives early (hence Worm) usually around 10ish. Yes, that is early for Devon. Grub however never shows up until well after 11 and sometimes not before 12. I can't start work until Grub has been. The reason he is late is because he stops at the top of our lane to have his breakfast. Can you imagine how infuriating this is? You know he's there. You know your post is with him. You know you can't start work until it's been. Better have lunch first and start afterwards. Sometimes there is no space between school run, waiting for the post, lunching, and then back to the afternoon school run. Before you know it the whole day has gone past in a long lazy nothingness.

And then there's the garden. Can you imagine, you there in your nice soft warm city office, what it is like to look out of your window and to be actually able to see the grass growing, hedges that need pruning, beds that need weeding and, oh bugger, the chickens have got out again. Back in a moment.

Now where was I? Oh yes. Looking out of the window simply reminds one of how much there is to do and I now prefer to work with my blinds down to shut out such distractions. Yes, what is the point of moving to the countryside only to shut it out? Yes, well, what is it then?

So between the kids and the friends and the distractions and the chickens escaping one has to be pretty disciplined, pretty damn dedicated. The countryside *can* inspire if it goes quiet for long enough. It can certainly set one off on dreamy trains of thought, but that doesn't get the deadlines met. And, oh yes, that wood burning stove that figured so largely in your dream. Well, someone has to chop logs for it. Guess who? Yep, you again, along with the mowing and the pruning and the weeding. Guess who will get their logs delivered, chopped and stacked? I know, I know. This wasn't part of the dream but your time will seem so tight you'll have to edit the dream a bit if you are to get any real work done.

The bottom line is: if you are going to move to the countryside to be creative and you aren't doing so now, then the chances are you aren't going to be any more creative after you've moved. Moving to the countryside can inspire you but it won't change your basic

personality. If you're not working at your chosen thing now then you have to ask yourself why not. To make your living at anything creative requires:

II Determination

II Discipline

II Experience

II Acquired skills

II Dedication

II Drive

You had better be sure you have these things in place before you move or you'll end up enjoying the scenery and not doing any work.

Once you are settled and working well you probably need to sell whatever it is you creatively produce. This is where living in the countryside may have drawbacks you might not have considered – well, you will now you've read this. For a start there is your market. No, not your farmer's market or the local fruit and veg market. I mean any outlet for your work. You may be much more limited in your choice of outlets and find that only by going back to the city can you find sufficient channels for sales.

This might mean more commuting than you were doing before. I have a friend who finds he has to go back to London rather more frequently than he envisaged. For us from Devon this is a six hour round trip. Pete has to do this twice a week – 12 hours a week. Previously he got the tube and it was a twenty minute trip – weekly commuting for him in London was about three and a half hours. Now he's doing three times that. Brilliant.

Of course moving to the country can indeed inspire you but only if you're already producing. Don't expect lush green fields to do the work for you. You still have to slog away but in a nicer place, that's all. On the other hand, there are times when the scenery takes your breath away. You wake to mist rising off the lake or a black night noticeable for the complete absence of street lights when you feel you can see every star in the Milky Way and you stand transfixed with an inaudible 'Oh God' on your lips. Yes, sometimes the countryside inspires you, awes you, grips you with its beauty, its wildness, its incredible romance. The sunrises and the sunsets are better than they ever were over factories and office buildings. And then in those moments you know why you made the move. Well done you.

PROS

The countryside can be a great place to find inspiration for creative work, whether paid or as a hobby.

It's far more stimulating working among green views and beautiful surroundings than in a grimy city (unless, I suppose, you paint grimy city landscapes).

CONS

The main downside is to do with motivation. If you can't find the motivation to be creative in the city, ther's a tendency to blame the surroundings. But in fact, well motivated people can work anywhere. If you can't get round to it now, chances are you'll fare no better in the country.

Following on from this, there are arguably more distractions in the country than there are in town, so even less tends to get done.

Finding outlets for creative work can be much tougher in the country than in town, and you may have to travel back to the city to sell your work.

KEY QUESTIONS

II Are you working productively where you are at the moment?

II If not, will the countryside honestly motivate you any better?

II How will you deal with distractions – visitors, post arriving late, school runs, the garden calling and all the rest?

II If you need to make money from your creative work, where and how will you sell it?

II Will you need to commute to a city to sell your work? Does this influence how far from the city you want to move?

———

Playing host to townie friends

THE DREAM

They motor down on a Friday evening and arrive around supper time. You are so pleased to see them and they come in to smiles and hugs and a decent bottle or two of red warming next to the Aga. Over supper you regale them with tales of your move and how you've settled in and everything that's happened to you since you moved. Their stories of city life seem pale and boring in comparison to yours.

The next day you take them on a tour of the local attractions and they talk of making the move themselves. By Sunday lunch, which is very long and lingering, they are serious and asking you to send them the local papers so they can look for houses near you. Late Sunday afternoon you wave them off and, as they motor back to the city, you settle back to have a look at the papers and sip a last glass or two. There's nothing to do as your delightful guests loaded the dishwasher before they left, made their beds and emptied the ashtrays. They were easy to have around, great company and you're looking forward to them coming again.

THE REALITY

If it is like that sometimes you will be lucky. Mostly you can't wait for them to go. They leave a bloody mess behind that takes you until Tuesday to clear up. When you knew your friends in the city you invariably met up with them for an evening. But the whole point about townie friends once you've moved to the country is that they stay for a whole weekend at a time. Suddenly you get to see them first thing in the morning...not pleasant. They have some very unsociable habits.

They arrive with kids and dogs and au pairs that you didn't know were coming. They suddenly seem very picky and faddy about food. They smoke in the bedroom. They insist on seeing all the local tourist attractions which you've seen every weekend since you moved. They mock you about moving to the sticks, instead of being suitably impressed. They seem bright and fun and young and you realise that living in the country has made you old fashioned, out of touch and drab. They won't go and are still there eating and drinking you out of house and home on Wednesday. You won't see them in the winter. They think you're a free B&B.

They say they'll turn up on Friday evening in time for supper but they actually arrive in the early hours of Saturday, crashing drunk, waking the kids and claiming the trains were delayed. Talking of trains, you spend the whole weekend driving them everywhere if they do come by train. God, weekend visitors are a nightmare. Entertain them? Yeah, sure, at first you might but you won't see them after a few visits. Or if you do they'll be a pain. They'll poke your fire and complain about how cold it is. They don't bring jumpers or wellies and expect you to provide them. They bring white and drink red – unforgivable. In fact, they bring cheap white and drink expensive red – even more unforgivable. They drink rather more of the expensive reds than you'd have thought possible.

The fact is that townie friends whom you used to socialise with for an evening will descend on you for a couple of days or more at a time. Sometimes several of them at a time. It's hard work, cooking every meal for several people for a weekend, preparing the beds, getting the shopping in, tidying up (at least a bit) and putting off your usual weekend activities.

Once they've arrived, you find your privacy is severely curtailed for 48 hours or so rather than just an evening, and you feel obliged to stay up every night until *they* want to go to bed, and be up in time to get them breakfast in the morning. We all have different styles of entertaining, but however laid back you are, weekend guests put paid to any ideas of a relaxing weekend for you. You'll be too busy giving *them* a relaxing weekend.

And it's expensive. A weekend shopping bill when you have friends staying – especially when you want to give them a good country weekend with a Sunday roast and plenty of apple pie and home cooking – can come to as much as your usual weekly shop when you're on your own.

You'll soon find that while some friends are always welcome, others quickly get to be a pain. They become boring after the first few hours, but you're stuck with them for another two days, and they simply don't pull their weight so you have endless clearing up to do after them. And then there are the ones who eat all your food and then disappear for the day, returning only for a slap-up supper at your expense. They just wanted a free weekend in the country, with all meals cooked and washing up done for them. You come to dread them visiting.

And, you see, there's a funny thing. People don't wait to be invited for a weekend in the country. The etiquette seems to be that they phone up and invite themselves to stay. I sometimes wonder if it isn't due to a feeling that they're doing you a favour –deigning to keep you in touch with civilisation. Saying no politely can be tricky, too, because they often ask, "When would be a good weekend for you?" Either you have to be rude, or you have to let them come.

Malcolm Muggeridge and his wife once stayed with friends for the weekend. They drove away after having said their farewells when Malcolm remembered they'd left their umbrella in the

front porch. Rather than disturb their friends his wife popped back to collect it and was startled to see their hosts in their sitting room doing a bizarre little dance which involved hopping from one foot to the other while waving their arms in the air and chanting 'they've gone, they've gone, they've gone, they've gone'. Good on Muggeridge for having the nerve to tell this story against himself.

Of course it's not always like this. Some friends will be an absolute delight and will clear up after themselves and be entertaining, helpful, friendly, suitably awed about your move, interested in what you are doing and it's brilliant to catch up on all the gossip. They offer to walk your dogs for you, look after your kids so you can have a nap after cooking that huge Sunday lunch, bring a decent red and some flowers, get a taxi back to the station after lunch and drop you a note to say thanks later in the week. That's perfection. If only it happened more often.

PROS

The best guests are a delight, and it's a treat to see them for a whole weekend instead of just for an evening.

It's great fun when friends visit your country house, applaud you for making the move, and admire your garden, your home, your surroundings and all the rest of it.

You can't beat a long, lazy Sunday lunch in the country, whether it's outdoors in the summer or in a steamy Aga-warm kitchen in winter.

CONS

Until you're subjected to your friends for 48 hours at a time, you can't always be sure which ones are still fun after two days continuously in their company.

It's hard work having weekend guests.

It's very expensive entertaining people in the style to which you would like them to think you have become accustomed.

Townies rarely have guests to stay over (except maybe crashing on the sofa when they've missed their last train home and are too drunk to ring for a taxi). This means they have no idea how much trouble they can be, so many of them fail to help with the cooking or washing up, leave a mess everywhere, bring extra children or dogs without warning, and don't contribute to the cost.

People will happily invite themselves to stay for a whole weekend, making it quite hard to avoid unwanted friends politely.

Some people find the lack of privacy and time to yourself, that goes with having people in your house for days at a time, difficult to cope with.

Some guests, quite frankly, exploit and abuse you, using you as a free B&B.

Even those who don't abuse you will still choose to visit in good weather, quite understandably. You may not see any of your townie friends all winter.

KEY QUESTIONS

II Are you used to having people stay for two or three days at a time? Do you know how much work is involved?

II How laid back are you about mess, clean sheets, smoking in bedrooms, leaving the washing up until morning and so on? The more particular you are about having things done your way, the more stressful you will find townie visitors.

II Are you happy to have a house full for days on end, or do you miss your privacy?

II Are you flush enough to keep paying for townie visitors? Some will contribute but others won't. Either way it will still cost you more than a weekend without visitors.

II How do you feel about being taken for granted/taken for a ride/exploited and abused? Is it worth it to see your friends? Or are you a happy martyr? Or will it frustrate and anger you?

II How assertive are you? To make this work, you may need to

be firm about house rules, or even tell certain people that you don't want them to visit overnight.

You can't stop people inviting themselves to stay, and you want to keep in touch with your friends. But if this aspect of country living doesn't appeal to you, would you be better off staying close enough to the city that friends can visit for the day rather than a whole weekend at a time?

———

A COTTAGE WITH ROSES ROUND THE DOOR

THE DREAM

Old. Probably thatched. Roses, sweet ambling, sweet smelling ones of course, around the door. Inside: leaded windows, stripped floorboards in oak trodden by the honest boots of English yeomen for a thousand years – and yeowomen and yeochildren of course. Tiny rooms lit by discreet table lamps reflecting polished wood and lots of chintz. Huge inglenooks that throw out masses of heat from open roaring log fires. An oak mantelpiece festooned with brass and a mirror above. The walls rough plastered with the odd watercolour picture of a local landscape. Overhead dark beams, thick, sturdy, oak. Strong stone flags underfoot.

Upstairs, tiny bedrooms with low sloping ceilings and dormer windows. Outside, a kitchen garden jam-packed with vegetables and soft fruit, and flower beds with hollyhocks, foxgloves, lady's mantle and love-in-a-mist. Somewhere a bonfire adds its smokey atmosphere and doves softly coo from the white painted dovecote. An ancient weather vane slowly turns to suggest the hint of a perfect breeze. All is well with the world and you, snug in your ancient cottage, feel smug and enhanced and happy.

THE REALITY

I think that even in that brief description you might already be able to see some of the distinct drawbacks this dream has. For a start, cottages were built for country folk. They earned their living out of doors during daylight hours. They had no need of windows as they were never at home during the day to need adequate light. And glass was expensive, so the smaller the windows, the cheaper they were. You'll find most cottages have tiny windows for this reason – and they kept the heat in.

Cottages are tricky to heat unless you install central heating – and then they lose a lot of their charm. Those big old inglenooks? No, they don't throw out much heat in a lot of cases; they throw out a lot of smoke and dust and ash and soot and dirt. Someone has to keep them well supplied with logs which generate a lot of heat, of which eighty percent immediately disappears straight up the chimney. This creates massive draughts as your tiny room struggles to produce enough oxygen to replace all the lovely hot air that has just vanished up the rickety old chimney. And the chimney needs sweeping twice a year and birds are forever falling down it, so you come down in the morning to soot all over the chintzy things and the polished wooden surfaces scratched by claws, and bird shit everywhere. Been there, done that.

If your cottage is listed or in a conservation area there's bugger all you can do to it without planning permission. Isobel and Nick, a couple I knew, had an ideal little cottage that needed a new roof as the nails had rotted away and the tiles were slipping. One council department said the roof had to be replaced at once as it was dangerous and another department said touch that roof at your peril, it's listed and in a conservation area and is a fine example of a clay pin tiled roof on an 18th century mill drying rooms cottage or some such baloney. I'm not unsympathetic but Isobel and Nick had to live in the blasted thing and they didn't know what to do for the best. Result: they let the two departments fight it out and moved.

Don't ever buy an old house without having a thorough survey done. They are usually sturdy overall, but they can have long term problems which are about to need expensive work. Reconstructing walls, putting in ties and replacing roofs are not cheap, and may be necessary. By the same token, there will almost always be persistent minor problems which you must learn to live with. It's no good expecting perfection. There will be a damp patch that nothing will get rid of, although you can keep it under control. There will be patches of plaster that flake in a modest way from time to time and would cost a fortune to replace. There will be a window where the rain comes in during really foul weather no matter what you do.

Oh, a quick word about thatch. It is expensive to replace; it could be as frequent as every ten years. Tricky to get insured at times. The squirrels love to nest in it – which gives them access to your attic space where they love to chew through your electric cables. And thatch catches fire more often than slate. You'll also get the grockles peering in through your windows all summer long if you're anywhere near a tourist trail.

If you are in the market for a cottage try and avoid the ones which have been tastefully 'done up'. This usually means some twit has installed double glazing, under floor heating, replaced all the wooden windows with white plastic ones, added on a conservatory, rebuilt the kitchen from Ikea, installed a Calor gas fire in the inglenook and converted the loft into a work-from-home-study complete with built in pine desk accessories and filing cabinets. Yuck. All you'll be getting is a modern box with a dark interior and a mucked about exterior.

When I say 'cottage', you can extend this to take in farmhouses, lodge houses, and pretty well anything in the country except mansions. Low beams mean tall people don't come and visit you too often – for tall read anyone over 5' 8". Old houses can be incredibly damp – built as they were long before damp proof courses were thought of. They are invariably expensive to buy –

you don't get a lot for your money except history – as you townies are all after them. And they can be incredibly expensive to maintain.

But on the positive side they are warm in the winter if you get the fireplace right, and cool in the summer. They create terrific talking points and give you instant heritage and history. They hold their charm no matter what is going on in the outside world – you come home to warmth and cosiness and snug protection. They were built to withstand storms and gales and wind and rain and anything the weather can throw at them. They've been there for five hundred years (or whatever) and will last another five hundred.

Yes, they may be expensive initially but you can always get your money back; they are a good investment and you know they aren't going to deteriorate alarmingly fast like a modern box will. Nor will they date (they will always be fashionably old fashioned). Since they are small they are easy to furnish and cheap to heat once you have the draughts under control. This is a dream that will never go out of style.

PROS

A country cottage is undoubtedly romantic and homely.

You really feel you're living your dream when you come home every day to a little cottage with roses round the door.

Old cottages can be very snug and warm once you get the heating right.

An old house is a good investment.

CONS

Little old cottages tend to be pretty dark inside. The earliest houses that are generally light and bright are Georgian houses, which have bigger windows.

Stone buildings are very cold until you've found out the best system for heating them. You may have to install central heating if the house doesn't already have it.

If your property is listed you may find that you're not even allowed to repaint the front door without permission.

Some old buildings can have very serious problems that previous owners have ignored, so you need a good survey.

You will need to learn to live with minor, non-structural problems such as damp patches and flaking plaster. You simply can't fix everything.

Think twice about thatch — it looks lovely but it is a big expense and a safety risk.

Low ceilings are a frequent characteristic of old houses. If you are tall, you may find it excruciatingly irritating never to be able to stand up straight in your own living room.

It is increasingly difficult to find unspoiled cottages these days. Most of them have been 'renovated' (for which read 'ruined') by country folk who couldn't give two hoots about the rural idyll but just want windows that let in light and don't let in draughts. The reason the cottage is now up for sale is that they're moving to a nice modern box.

KEY QUESTIONS

II Why do you want to live in a country cottage? What is it you're really after?

II What period of property do you want? Why?

II Do you have stipulations about thatch, ceiling height, size of windows, light levels and so on? It helps to think these things through and give yourself (and the estate agents) guidelines before you start house-hunting.

II Listed buildings are generally very attractive, and of course they have a cachet, but they also restrict what alterations you can make. Do you want to look for, or avoid, listed buildings?

II Are you happy to put up with minor damp patches and the like, draughts, and higher dust levels than a modern house? If not, would you be better off looking for something new, or a halfway point such as a late Victorian or Edwardian house?

=

MAKING YOUR OWN JAM

THE DREAM

In your huge kitchen warmed by your Aga you stand surrounded by lots of freshly washed jam jars. On the range, bubbling quietly, there is a vast pan of simmering fruit. The kids have been in tasting and helping. You have been writing out some labels and have a list of all your lovely relatives who will be looking forward to their annual Christmas gift of home made jam from nature's stores. The smell is indescribably rich and sweet and gorgeous. The taste is so pleasurable that people have been known to explode eating less nice things. And you grew all the fruit yourself, lovingly, carefully.

This is what you moved to the country for: jam making, bread baking, pickling, storing, marinating, curing and saving, jugging, preserving, bottling, smoking, making use of the harvest, the surplus left over from a rich spring, summer and autumn of gardening. The colours are so deep and lush; reds and purples and greens and golds and scarlets. There is nothing more rewarding than looking in your larder and seeing rows of neat jars all labelled and waiting for the depths of the winter when you can bring them forth and enjoy again the taste of summer.

On the other hand those relatives might not be quite so happy to get a jar of your home made again. They might be heartily sick of your green tomato chutney, your bramble offerings and your jars of sour marmalade. You too might not find the experience quite so romantic, so perfect as you thought. The kids won't help, even if they think they are. It is a lot of hard work. That glut you anticipated might not even happen if the birds get there first. The kitchen seems hot and steamy and there are so many other things to do.

All the jam you made now has a thin layer of mould on it. The labels all fell off and you haven't a clue what's what. Anyway, nothing is so fattening as home made jam – have you any idea how much sugar you'll need? And there's you starting another diet.

If you try to sell any of your produce you'll encounter the wonderful world of EU legislation – do you really want to invest thousands in a scrubbed down, stainless steel, hygienic, sterile, disinfected, smelling strongly of carbolic, inspected weekly, germ-free, sanitised kitchen? I thought not. But even cooking jam for the WI fair is now subject to health and safety legislation.

While there are undoubtedly more expensive hobbies (take a look at the section on keeping a horse), preserving food isn't as cheap as you might think. You need giant preserving pans, jars of various kinds, and all those labels/rings of greaseproof paper/circles of gingham to tie round the top. Not expensive individually, perhaps, but it all adds up. And preserves such as chutneys need all sorts of ingredients you don't grow in your garden to add to the free ones you do.

And think of the washing up afterwards. And the lingering sweet smell that hangs about for weeks. And the wasps that'll get you when you are out there picking up windfalls. And it's so much cheaper to buy jam and bread and pickles and preserves from the supermarket, don't you think? No? Still game? Good. Here's the upside.

You'll be using fresh, organic, healthy ingredients – apart from the sugar but then pleasure isn't something you can ration. A little of what you fancy is never enough. You will probably be able to get rid of any surplus you make down at the local farmers' market or the WI; they usually turn a blind eye to regulations. You'll be pursuing a very traditional occupation that will put you in touch with the heart of country living very quickly. Baking bread and making jam and preserving pickles and all that stuff fills your home with wonderful smells, love, warmth, helping friends, jars of wonderful tastes and waiting energy.

You'll be making good use of any windfalls, glut, surpluses and not wasting the bounteous harvest of nature. You'll be busy and happy. It helps you improve your cooking skills and anyone in their right mind would be glad of your gift of home-made jam. But the biggest plus point is you get to control what goes in. You get to pick the fruit, make the jam, add the ingredients. You know what you and your family are eating and that's important. Making jam is terribly satisfying.

PROS

If you enjoy cooking, making preserves and baking bread is great fun.

Jams and chutneys, home made bread and cakes, all smell wonderful while they're cooking.

You can make sure there's no waste of food in your garden – every last piece of fruit and windfall can be used up.

You're in control of what goes into the food your family eats.

CONS

It's not easy to find the time to make bread regularly, or a few big batches of preserves every autumn.

If your enthusiasm – or cooking skill – falters, you can be left with a lot of jars of

mouldy food. Jam today is fine, but jam tomorrow... and the day after, and the day after that?

It's very messy and creates a lot of washing up and tidying away.

It's not as cheap as you might think, making your own jams and pickles and so on.

You have to find somewhere to store all those jars, both before and after you've filled them.

If you want to sell your produce you are technically subject to health and safety legislation and should have your kitchen inspected.

KEY QUESTIONS

II Are you a keen cook at the moment? If so, fine. If not, are you sure you're likely to turn into one just because you move to the country?

II Making jams and pickles and chutneys needs to be done in large quantities. This takes a lot of time and generates a lot of mess and washing up. Not everyone has time for this. If you have a job and a family or a busy lifestyle of some other kind, are you sure you're going to have time?

II Who is going to eat this stuff?

Driving a Landrover/Tractor

THE DREAM

Imagine a winding hill with a gently disappearing lane in the soft evening sunshine. And there's you bumbling along in your old Series 1 Landrover. As the sun sets you meander along towards home. You park up under the shelter of an old barn and it's time for tea; time to light the wood burning stove and time to pore over those wonderful catalogues of parts for your vintage tractor which snuggles cosily alongside the Landrover outside in the barn. Tomorrow you will mow the bottom field. Tomorrow you may take Betsy to the local garage where, with shiny eyes, they will lovingly chew the fat with you about her and about her restoration which you are going to do over the next few years. They just love to stop and talk Landrover with recently moved townies.

THE REALITY

Get a grip. In the country you are known, and not particularly affectionately, as a Bickie. No, it's nothing to do with biscuits. It means Big Income, Cheap Car. And they don't like it one bit. If it was up to them all those old Landrovers would have been pensioned off years ago and we'd all be driving those nice new Japanese 4x4s. And you paid what for it? Oh, how they laugh.

As townies many of us have this dream of driving lovely vintage machinery and living in old cottages. In the country they yearn for modern air-conditioned cars and houses. They've had generations of making do, mending, repairing, doing without, envying and they think we are, to put it bluntly, bloody nuts for wanting to keep all this old stuff going when it is obviously redundant, outmoded, old fashioned and out of date. They hate rust. They loathe our affection for antique machinery and they don't want to talk about it at all.

Downside. Yes, there has to be one. You can't get parts easily. In fact sometimes you can't get your local garage to even look at it let alone repair it and yes, they have gone over to computers and modern Euroboxes.

If your vehicle is past its best, you can't just bumble along; traffic won't tolerate it and they do have horns, various finger signs which are universal and lots of unpleasant sounding country words. Old vehicles break down a lot and the AA/RAC will only give you so many breakdowns a year now before you get struck off/penalised/talked to sharply.

Old vehicles don't go through MoTs very well, and country garages are fed up to the back teeth with townies saying 'Oh, give the old girl another year, she's worth it, they don't make 'em like this any more'. No, and the reason they don't is because they were crap at the time. A modern Landrover is reliable, warm, doesn't leak or spew oil, it's comfortable and cheap to run. The old ones are draughty, expensive to run, unreliable and smelly.

Modern farmers use modern tractors and modern machinery. The reason is very easy to understand. The modern stuff is reliable, efficient and easy to maintain. To have you turn up banging on about how your TVO[1] Ferguson from 1952 is a wonderful old grey Fergie and she'll outlive all this modern junk, won't win you any brownie points. If modern farmers suffered

[1] Tractor Vapourising Oil – now redundant but you can make it using a mix of diesel, petrol and/or paraffin. Email me and I'll send you the recipe. Yep, I've got one. Bloody townie.

from such nostalgia they would go bust faster than they are going anyway.

I know that when we go on holiday we drive through the countryside and invariably encounter an old farmer driving an old tractor that can't possibly be road legal with a whole gaggle of cars behind while he tows a ton or two of hay on a rickety trailer obviously made pre-war to take only half a ton max. But these farmers are a dying breed. There is no reason to join them. Except of course a love of old machinery.

The upside? If you have the time there is a wonderful glut of hidden scrap yards where you can happily salvage for hours for all the bits you'll need. And as well as enjoying your vehicle on your own, there are lots of other townies who will be happy to talk old machinery with you. They won't laugh and say 'You paid what for it?!' when you've just bought a 1953 three cylinder diesel Massey Ferguson that no one in the countryside would touch with a barge pole[2].

And the Internet means there are lots of newsgroups who will give you advice, help, information, email you workshop manuals and such like. Lots of other vintage tractor enthusiasts out there for you to play with. Mail order means you get parts delivered to your door so you don't have to risk the sniggering down at your local garage when you go in and inadvertently ask for the wrong bit, or make the mistake of calling a rounded shank cotter pin the giggle pin, or the wotsit pin that goes in the thingummy.

You can also reassure yourself with the knowledge that you are helping to protect and preserve a valuable heritage – and one that would, by rights, entirely disappear if left to the very people who cut their teeth on it originally.

---

[2] They are notoriously unreliable starters (the tractors, not the barge poles).

And best of all, you'll just have so much fun playing around with big bits of metal that make lots of lovely loud noises. Maybe it's a boy thing.

PROS

You can buy old vehicles pretty cheaply, and many of them are even exempt from road tax.

So long as you avoid country folk and local garages, you'll find plenty of townie friends eager to talk about your old bits of metal with you.

If you're on the Net, you can access advice, information and even parts pretty easily.

Any 4WD is genuinely useful in the country (as opposed to the town, where it simply makes you look like a prat).

CONS

It's often difficult to get parts.

Old vehicles are more prone to break down. Yes, even Landrovers.

You'll stand out a mile as a townie, and your local garage won't let you forget it.

KEY QUESTIONS

II What kind of vehicle do you want?

II How easy is it to get parts for?

II How reliable is it likely to be (be honest here)? How essential is it to have it in working order? If it's the only vehicle for getting to work, or the tractor is vital for the 10-acre smallholding you're buying, best get something that won't break down.

Peace and quiet

THE DREAM

You move away from the hurly-burly, the noise, the late night par-tying, the slamming of car doors at two in the morning, the roar of the traffic, the screaming of sirens – and it is all tranquil and quiet. You can hear a pin drop, perhaps a little gentle bird song, a cuckoo calling, the far away tap of a woodpecker, doves cooing, the gentle sighing of the grass growing. All is still and quiet and peaceful.

THE REALITY

In your dreams perhaps. Listen, you can live in the depths of the countryside, as far away from a road as it's possible to get and do you know what? You'll discover this dream of peace and quiet is a myth. All day long you'll have to listen to:

- Tractors
- Jets overhead using your corner of the countryside as a train-ing run for bombing missions
- Sheep baa-ing
- Geese honking

- Cows

- Horses

- Dogs barking

- Wind – the correct word round here is 'hooning' and by golly it hoons at you in the winter

- Rain

Yes, it might be quiet if the countryside would shut up for a moment. You don't get peace and quiet; you get a swap – tractors for cars, cows for buses, that sort of thing. Yes, there is no roar of traffic but there is, certainly in the spring, the roar of randy bulls that somehow echoes across the valleys for miles and starts incredibly early in the mornings.

And have you any idea what time farmers get up? No, I thought not. I'll just say it is very early. Very, very early. Earlier than you would have thought legal. I think the bulls wake them – or is it the sheep or the cockerels or the geese? And in late summer when the grass is being cut for silage I've known tractors out there still working past midnight. You see their headlights on in places where vehicles don't normally appear, like giant ghostly cows haunting the hillsides – spooky and noisy.

Have you any idea what time cockerels get up? Again, I thought not. Before moving to the country I assumed they crowed to tell someone, anyone, that it was dawn. So why do they crow at one in the morning when daylight is still some hours away? No, I don't know either but I do love snuggling down to sleep and hearing it. Makes me want to get up straightaway.

If you are expecting quiet, do a little research before you move to your dream cottage. Enquire what farms are nearby. My brother moved to rural Wales and discovered his cottage overlooked the local cathedral town complete with cathedral. When the wind was in the wrong direction you couldn't hear yourself talk at his place because of the bell ringing on a Wednesday evening. The bell ringers locked themselves into their tower because someone had gone for them with an axe sometime in the past. I could completely understand that and so could my brother. How did my brother know they locked the door? You only get one guess here.

Someone once gave me the advice that you should park up near your chosen new home before you complete the purchase and just sit and listen and watch. Do this at odd random times of the day – and different days of the week. You'll be surprised at what you find out; stuff that doesn't appear on any estate agent's particulars. I, of course, have never actually done this which is why I bought a cottage next door to the village pub. It was indeed a quiet pub when there were customers in there. But very early in the morning the brewery delivered and you have no idea how noisy those barrels are when dropped off the back of a lorry onto the tarmac. Not to mention the noise, the drunks and the car doors slamming at closing time.

I also inherited cockroaches from the pub and every bank holiday my garden became a litter bin for the local ramblers association who met at the pub before setting off on their rambling. They would all sit along my garden wall and eat their picnic lunches and throw the detritus into my garden. Great. I loved it. I thought it added a little local colour to my previously humdrum city life.

Wendy and Trevor bought a house in a quiet market town. They only saw the house when house hunting at weekends when the road was quiet and the house delightfully peaceful. They bought and duly moved in. On the first Monday morning they were horrified by the roar of traffic that stopped outside the house. Yep, they had bought in the road which was used as the town car park by all the shop workers, the tourist office, the post office staff, even the school staff. They found they were looking out on a sea of cars. Then, from about 3pm onwards, it was slam, slam, slam as drivers drove off and the road only reverted to silence after about six when everyone was gone.

But it's not all bad. Yes, it can be incredibly noisy but there are also some evenings when the air is so still and everything seems suspended, motionless, caught in a perfect moment of utter peace and quiet and it takes your breath away. There are mornings when nothing moves, nothing moos or cries or honks and you stand looking out totally enchanted by the perfect peace.

PROS

When it actually does go quiet, the countryside is infinitely quieter than the city will ever be.

In the country, you don't get that frenetic buzz that often comes with city life.

Many (though not all) country noises are pleasant to listen to and can even be therapeutic: waves washing on the shingle, rooks cawing, sheep bleating and so on.

CONS

Some parts of the countryside are as noisy as any city, with trains, jets, farm machinery and so on shattering the silence frequently.

If you live near a farm, it can be very noisy from early morning to late at night. And farmers are one of those groups of people that feel they have special rights — they're not going to cut silage earlier or later in the day just to keep you happy.

Farm animals, most notoriously cockerels, start getting noisy by dawn *at the latest*. In summer, that can mean half past three in the morning.

Church bells may be delightful wafting over the meadow on a sunny Sunday morning. But if you live next door to the church they can drive you mad every Wednesday evening (or whenever), especially if you're trying to get the kids to sleep.

Think twice before you buy close to the village pub. However handy you think it will be on the evenings when you're visiting it, it can be a major disturbance every other night.

Traffic travels fast and noisily on country roads. Roads that are quiet in the evenings and at weekends, can mutate into snarling highways between 8am and 6pm on a weekday. And quiet rural spots that you visit in winter may be crawling with tourists in the summer months.

KEY QUESTIONS

Is the house you're thinking of buying close to any of the following?

II a farm

II a church

II a pub

II a road

II a tourist spot

If so, you need to check out how much noise this tends to generate, at all times of the day, the week and the year.

Try visiting your chosen property at different times and just standing outside to listen. OK, the locals will think you're mad, but they think that about all townies anyway, so you've nothing to lose.

———

———

WHAT PEOPLE SAY ABOUT LIVING IN THE COUNTRY

We ran a survey before writing this book to find out what dreams people have about living in the country. The topics I've covered in this book have been chosen on the basis of their responses, but we asked other questions too and I thought you might like to see what they said.

WHO DID WE SURVEY?

We surveyed just over a hundred people around the UK, a third of them townies and two-thirds ex-townies, living as far apart as Scotland, Cornwall and London. We decided to send batches of survey forms to friends and contacts around the country and ask them to pass them on to other people, either ex-townies or townies dreaming of moving out. We chose this method because we didn't want to use a route that would bias the results. For example, if we'd asked local ramblers groups to distribute forms, we'd have got a disproportionately high number of ticks beside 'going for long walks'. Sending out forms to smallholders groups would have led to too many ticks for 'growing your own vegetables' and 'keeping chickens'. As it is, we believe the responses are as unbiased as possible.

Interestingly, after the first 90 percent of results came in we

analysed them to see which dreams were coming out tops. After the final ten percent of forms came back, we added these to the results and found that the running order was completely unchanged. In other words, we felt any subsequent responses were simply echoing what we had already learned.

SO WHAT WERE THEIR FAVOURITE DREAMS?

We listed 32 fantasies about country life, assembled from our own experience and by talking to various people, and asked each respondent to tick three or four on the list that they personally dreamed of before they moved. Or still dream of in the case of those aspiring country-dwellers who hadn't yet made the move. The following list shows what percentage of the total respondents ticked each dream. Since they all ticked more than one, the totals add up to a lot more than 100 percent – sorry if I'm teaching my grandmother to suck eggs here (perhaps another country pursuit?).

We took all the dreams chosen by 5 percent or more of respondents for this book. I've rounded up the figures to whole numbers here to make it easy to follow.

Dream	% respondents
Having space and wide views	58
Healthy environment and fresh air	50
The change to a slower pace of life	31
Going for long walks	30
Having a big garden	26
Being part of a community	25
Being near trees and wildflowers	24
Being near water	21
Somewhere safe to bring up kids	21
Growing your own vegetables	18
Having a big kitchen with an Aga	17
Being aware of the seasons passing	17
Getting back to nature	17

Having open fires or woodburners	15
Sending the kids to a better school	12
Keeping chickens	10
Keeping a horse	10
Doing up an old barn	9
A creative place to write or paint	8
Playing host to townie friends	8
A cottage with roses round the door	6
Making your own jam etc	5
Driving a landrover/tractor etc	5
Being able to hunt, shoot or fish	3
Keeping ducks	2
Keeping sheep	2
Keeping goats	2
Keeping pigs	2
Keeping bees	1
Being able to dress the part	1
Running a b&b or guest house	1
Doing pottery or country crafts	0

WHAT DID WE MISS?

We're not infallible; we may have missed something important off the list. But at least we were aware of this so we gave our respondents an 'other' box to add dreams we'd failed to list. Several points were mentioned by only one respondent each, and several were not so much dreams as simply plus points. For example, one person mentioned lower insurance – arguably a valid point but surely not a fantasy you lie in bed in your poky city bedroom dreaming of.

However, the one thing we did feel we'd missed, which was mentioned by four of our respondents, was peace and quiet, so we included this in the book too.

DOES THE REALITY MATCH THE DREAM?

We asked this question of all those who had made the move (67 of them). On a scale of 1 to ten, how closely does the reality live up to the dream?

If you're planning to move to the country, the news is good. Even those people with reservations about moving (which showed up in the answers we'll look at in a moment) didn't regret making the change. Seventy-two percent of respondents gave country living eight out of ten or above, and no one scored it below four. Here are the scores out of ten, and the percentage of people who gave each score.

Score out of 10	% of respondents
1	0
2	0
3	0
4	1
5	8
6	11
7	8
8	23
9	16
10	33

WHAT WOULD THE EX-TOWNIES DO DIFFERENTLY NEXT TIME?

We gave no clues here, so they had to think for themselves. We only allowed space on the form for one or maybe two points, so these will be the key mistakes that people feel they made. Without clues, there was obviously a wide variety of answers; encouragingly, 25 percent of ex-townies said they would do little or nothing differently next time. Of the three-quarters who did feel there might have been a better way, here are the changes that were mentioned by more than one respondent.

Do differently	No. of mentions
Get further from the beaten track	4
Move to a bigger village with better amenities	4
Move nearer the sea	3
Move sooner/when younger	3
Buy a larger property	3
Buy less land	2
Be self-employed	2

The lesson seems to be that it's important to think very clearly about what you really want, and in particular what you will still want when you get there. While acres of land, for example, are hugely appealing when you're stuck in the city, the work involved in maintaining them may not seem worth it once you're happily ensconced in the wide open spaces.

When we first moved to Devon (from London but via rural villages and towns) we didn't want to be too isolated. This house, in a tiny hamlet, seemed ideal. Within months, however, we had got so used to the seclusion that we have quite resented having neighbours ever since. I should add that we have only two neighbours, both very pleasant and self-contained, and only one of the houses is even visible from ours.

Some people aim to rent for a few months before buying, or move again after the first few years, either of which is ideal if you're not sure what you want. And the aim of this book, of course, is help you analyse what is and isn't right for you.

Some of the comments which were made by only one person are worth mentioning as they imply lessons that could apply to many aspiring country-dwellers. Some were clearly personal ('move to Scotland') but the following seem worth passing on. In no particular order:

II Plan ahead more
II Buy not rent

II Buy an old property
II Have my own car
II Buy a place that's already converted
II Make more money before moving
II Keep a flat in London
II Sell the flat in London

...and my personal favourite response to this question: 'Live further away from relatives'.

SO WHAT'S THE DOWNSIDE OF RURAL LIVING THEN?

There have to be downsides, too. The rest of this book has been about the dreams of rural existence, but what about the aspects that never make it into your dreams, for good reason? If you haven't yet moved to the country, it's as well to be forewarned about the negatives. I hope these don't put you off, but they should encourage you to think realistically about what kind of country lifestyle will suit you.

You may feel confident that some of these downsides won't bother you, but there will be some that you will care about, and a bit of forward planning can minimise them. For example, if like almost a quarter of our respondents you wouldn't be happy without shops and amenities to hand, you should be looking for a property in a large village or close to a town.

Again, this was an open question with no clues, so the answers had scope to vary widely. Interestingly, you'll see that the top few answers scored a high number of hits. Here is the percentage of respondents who mentioned each downside. (Some mentioned none and others several, so the percentages don't add up to anything in particular, let alone 100.)

Downside	% of respondents
Transport	25
Lack of amenities/shops etc	24
Social life is harder	10
Lack of culture	10
Country roads	9
Hard to find work/earn enough	7
Having to travel to town sometimes	6
Other townies	4
Everyone knows your business	3
Mud	3
Farms	3
Bleakness of winter	3
Missing family and friends	3
No recycling facilities	1
Grockles	1
Lack of broadband technology	1
Midges, mosquitoes and mice	1

Some of these speak for themselves, but others are worth discussing briefly. Working down in order of how often they were mentioned, here are the biggest downsides you should be warned about before you give up your clean city house with its local shops and public transport on hand, where your friends live just down the road and you're wonderfully anonymous when you want to be.

TRANSPORT

This particular downside might be better termed 'What transport?' You may recall that one of the respondents answered the question, 'What would you do differently next time?' with the reply 'Have my own car.' How right they were. Public transport ranges from the useless to the non-existent in almost all rural

areas. If you don't have a car you need to be either rich enough to take taxis everywhere or a very keen cyclist or, ideally, agoraphobic.

Simply going out for the evening means that, since you have to return by car, someone has to stay sober enough to drive. Either that or you only ever go out to your own village pub, on foot.

Travelling by car can take hours in some parts of the country. Maps give you miles but not minutes, and distances can be misleading. In some places you'll be lucky to get above 20 mph even on what look like major roads if the map were to be believed.

If you don't drive, you will almost certainly need to be in a large village with shops and a good bus service (check this out in advance). Even large villages may have only one bus a day to and from the local town. You may be better off on the outskirts of a small market town. Towns with mainline stations are ideal for access to cities, but you will find that house prices rise in the catchment area of these towns.

Even if you do have a car, the lack of transport is still a big change from the city. This is because you have to use the car so often. Unless you're in a village with a shop, you'll need a car every time you run out of milk. Even with a local village shop, you need a car if you run out of milk after 5.30pm...

LACK OF AMENITIES

...which leads us to the lack of amenities. Shops are the biggest amenity bugbear according to our survey. Even if you have a local shop which sells milk up to 5.30 (except on Wednesday afternoons, Sundays and days when Phyllis is feeling a bit under the weather) you're unlikely to have the range of clothes shops, department stores, furnishing stores and so on that you're used to in the city. Given the dire state of the public transport, you'll have to drive to your nearest city for any decent shopping.

The local town will probably have a WH Smith, a Woolworths, a Boots and the usual DIY stores. And one small department store. The one decent shop you should find is a supermarket in the local town. Most of the towns have a reasonable sized Tesco, Safeway, Waitrose or Asda.

It's not only shops, of course. Moving to the country you'll have to get used to only one post (often as late as midday), and post offices which close at 4.30pm (and Wednesday afternoons, Sundays and days when Phyllis is feeling a bit under the weather). There may be no newspaper or dairy deliveries if you're off the beaten track. Your nearest gym or swimming pool may be dozens of miles away, the local school could be 10 miles or more, and the choice of places to eat out – other than pubs – will be severely limited.

Ex-townies generally get used to this in the end, but it can take years to adapt fully, and there'll probably be the occasional bugbear that never leaves you. I personally have never stopped getting murderously frustrated when the post still hasn't turned up by 11.00am.

SOCIAL LIFE IS HARDER

It can be far harder to make friends in the country. It's just more difficult to get out and meet people. It's certainly possible, and after a few years you'll have plenty of friends assuming you get out and about (and aren't so ghastly no one wants to know you). But it does take longer than in the city.

If you're in a village you can get involved in the local community. Trouble is, it's full of the kind of people who live in villages and get involved. I'm not knocking these people at all, but they're not the kind of people you're used to in the big smoke, and they may not be soulmates. The thing is, by and large it's the ex-townies you'll get on best with, even if you hate yourself for it. And they are harder to find.

That old transport thing comes in again here. You need a car to get out and socialise. And once you've made good friends, you can't share a drink with them because your only way of getting home is by driving. So be prepared to take some time to build up a good circle of friends, and expect to get out and about, and join local groups and organisations, in order to meet them.

LACK OF CULTURE

Cinemas aren't too difficult to find in the country. Some are old and quaint, others are state-of-the-art multiplex giants. What are harder to come by are decent theatres, concert halls, art galleries and so on. Essentially, if you want culture you're going to have to visit the cities for it. Some lucky rural areas have a great arts centre or film theatre, but they're relatively rare and you won't get more than one in your area.

On the plus side, you'll find plenty of stately homes and beautiful gardens instead. And you'll also be able to enjoy the rural alternatives to culture: country shows, vintage tractor displays, town fairs, regattas and village fêtes. They may not be high culture, but they're a fun enertainment you won't find in the city.

COUNTRY ROADS

Now here's something that takes some getting used to. And judging by the responses to our survey, many ex-townies have never really been happy about finding room in their lives for country roads.

The most common complaints involve the danger (especially if you or your children cycle), the lack of gritting in the winter, and the tractors you get stuck behind. The idea of waiting for a herd of cows to mooch past as they go to milking sounds very romantic as you sit dreaming in your stinky, dirty city home. But apart from the fact that cows are just as stinky and dirty as any city home, they are also an infuriating delay when you're late to pick the kids up from school, or you're about to miss the train up to town (where you don't want to go anyway).

Country roads vary, of course, and if you're a nervous driver you'd be better off in East Anglia than in Cumbria, for example. And if you can't reverse, stay away from south Devon; at least my bit of it. People who can't back up in narrow lanes are perhaps the most infuriating thing of all about country roads to those of us who live in areas where the hedges are high and the lanes twisty. I once backed up for a neighbour who wound down her window and said, "Thank you! The last person who lived in your house couldn't reverse, and the one before wouldn't!"

I know one woman who used to get so pissed off by a particular lorry driver she encountered every morning on the way to work, and who always tried to make her do the backing up, that she decided to try a new strategy. One morning, as he sat there refusing to reverse, she turned off the engine, took the keys out of the ignition and dangled them at him through the window. His response was to turn his engine off, pick up a newspaper from the dashboard and start reading it.

That's enough about country lanes. Once I get started on the etiquette of reversing...

HARD TO FIND WORK/EARN ENOUGH

This pretty much speaks for itself. You need to recognise that work is harder to come by in many rural areas, especially if you don't want to travel miles for it (which is expensive). Salaries are lower than for the equivalent jobs in cities as a rule too. If you can telework/freelance or find some variation on that theme, this is often the best solution for townies escaping the rat race.

HAVING TO TRAVEL TO TOWN SOMETIMES

It's amazing how much you can resent the occasional visit to somewhere that, until recently, you had put up with full time.

Trips up to town are actually a bonus to some ex-townies, giving the occasional buzz of a kind of vibrancy you don't get in the country, and reminding you why it was so clever of you to leave. Many other ex-townies feel, however, that having left they should be able to stay gone and they don't appreciate having to return even briefly.

So why do you have to go back? Some people don't, of course. But many people find that the most effective way to earn a living in the country involves keeping a link with the city. Maybe you relocate or telework for the same employer you've been with in the city, or perhaps you freelance or start a business with clients or customers in the city. Or perhaps you simply can't tear yourself away from the shops and the theatres that easily and need to return for the occasional fix.

You may have to resign yourself to visits to town for these reasons or others. If this is going to be the case, it's as well to think about the commuting distance before you move out. Be realistic about how frequently you'll need to go up to town, and check out how long the trains take and how often they go, or what the driving time is.

OTHER TOWNIES

Yes, believe it or not, other townies who have moved out are popular hate figures in rural parts. It's worth knowing why, so that you don't become one of them, ostracised by your own kind. What many ex-townies abhor is other people who move into the country and suburbanise it. They start mowing verges that used to be full of nettles and valerian – and consequently butterflies. Then they dig up bits of the newly sanitised verge and plant petunias in it. Next, they get onto the parish council and start proposing that everyone else be made to 'tidy' their verges. And keep their cats under control. Then they campaign to get the green lanes properly surfaced, and for everyone in the village to have matching wheelie bins.

This kind of townie wants to tidy up the countryside and make it look like suburbia and, what's worse, they want to make everyone else do the same. If you are this kind of person yourself, my best advice to you is stay in the city and leave the rest of us alone (not that I'm biased you understand).

EVERYONE KNOWS YOUR BUSINESS

I had a friend when I was a teenager who lived in a country village. He told me about an occasion when he wanted to phone his girlfriend. Since the phone was in the front hall and he didn't really want his mother eavesdropping he decided to call from the phone box on the corner. He only chatted for about ten minutes but, by the time he got home, three people had visited his mother to let her know what he was doing, under the guise of enquiring whether the phone was faulty.

That's par for the course in the country. The postman – who is on first name terms with everyone in the village – will examine your post before dropping it on the mat. Your neighbours will peer through your windows, your garage mechanic will discuss the rubbish under your car seats with anyone who passes, and Phyllis in the shop will know more about you than you do yourself.

This is something you will simply have to put up with. You can keep to yourself, but avoid getting a reputation for being aloof or secretive, as this won't go down well. You're expected to be open about what you're up to – everyone else is. You'll be seen as snooty and stand-offish if you're too private, especially being a townie and an outsider.

So the moral is: if you're thinking of having an affair, don't move into a village.

MUD

It's everywhere in the winter. If you care how your car looks

you'll have to wash it not only on Sundays but on Mondays, Wednesdays and Fridays too. Or do what the rest of us do and give up; just put it through a car wash twice a year before the registration number becomes so invisible it's illegal.

And what about keeping dogs? In the country, even a five minute walk will mean bringing home a dog with more mud than fur. Either you have to clean the dog constantly, or you have to keep it in the porch or some room designated for the purpose. In the winter, all your clothes will get muddy – just getting in and out of the car will make them muddy. By about February it gets quite depressing.

FARMS

Now here's an interesting one. Yes, some townies actually have the gall to move to the country and then complain that it has farms in it. It's worth knowing, however, that farms aren't all fluffy lambs and rosy-cheeked farmers wives who bake apple cake all day long. They are filthy, noisy places, which frequently smell disgusting (think pigs, think muck-spreading), many of which are owned by farmers who spray chemicals you don't even want to think about all over the place.

From about half a mile away, the smell is probably the only thing that will really get to you. You might want to think twice before you move next door to a farm. If you're one of the nine percent of people who is enticed by the idea of doing up an old barn, remember that they are all located on or near farms, for obvious reasons.

BLEAKNESS OF WINTER

Winter in the country simply doesn't compare to winter in the city. It's so much more obvious. Of course brisk walks on frosty mornings are beautiful, and stomping home through the snowy dusk to hot cocoa and crumpets likewise, but days like these are few and far between.

Mostly it rains. The wind is freezing and simply getting from the front door to the car is deeply unpleasant. It really is wise to check out your dream country location in February as well as in July; it may be very different. You need to be especially wary of houses or villages near the sea, in areas with high rainfall, and in windswept and exposed places.

Be aware too that winter lasts a lot longer in the north than it does in the south. A bleak winter may mean a bleak eight months every year in the more northerly parts of Britain. Are you really sure this is what you want?

MISSING FAMILY AND FRIENDS

You'll have lots of visitors when you first move to the country, but it rarely lasts. They're less likely to visit in the winter than the summer (why bother, when in a few short months they can visit and get the benefit of the countryside in sunshine as well?). And they will get used to your absence and fill the gap with other friends. You'll keep the best friends of course, and the family, but you may find it tough getting used to seeing them for a weekend every couple of months when you were used to seeing them every week, even if only for an evening.

This is unavoidable, although it will take a while for the visits to fall off and, of course, you may well be delighted to lose some of your 'friends'. The important thing is to be aware of it, so at least you aren't surprised and hurt when it happens. In time you'll make new friends closer to your new home, and all will be well again.

NO RECYCLING FACILITIES

Only one respondent mentioned this, and I don't know how many people would care enough to list it as the single biggest downside of living in the country. All I can say is that almost

every small town has recycling facilities and this is only likely to be a problem if you live well off the beaten track.

GROCKLES

Although only one respondent mentioned this, it does get moaned about a lot in many rural areas. Grockles – tourists down from the towns – are a problem in some areas which are popular tourist destinations. The West Country, Cumbria, the Yorkshire Dales... these places and others are not designed to take the level of traffic that passes through them in the summer.

It is galling to move out of the city only to find yourself sitting in a twenty minute traffic jam in the middle of rural Dorset or Suffolk every time you take your kids to school, or nip out to the supermarket.

If you're planning to move to a tourist spot, ask around and find out where the heavy traffic is over the summer. You don't want it outside your front door.

LACK OF BROADBAND TECHNOLOGY

Again, only one respondent considered this significant enough to list as a major downside, but boy is it a popular gripe in rural villages. It could be years before many areas get broadband, and simply being on the edge of a small town rather than in a nearby village could make the difference. Bigger exchanges get connected sooner. So if it's important to you, check it out before you finalise where to live.

MIDGES, MOSQUITOES AND MICE

It's true that nature seems much closer in the country than it does in the big city. I know you're never more than three inches from a rat anywhere in the known universe, or whatever that statistic is, but you're much more aware of it in the country. My brother's London cat used to be in the habit of bringing home half-eaten pizzas and chicken carcasses, while country cats bring back squirrels, rabbits and even snakes.

If you live off the beaten track, you will encounter frequent spiders in the sitting room, bats in the bedroom, birds in the bathroom and woodlice everywhere. Many people regard this as a positive plus to living in the countryside, but others don't like it at all. And I've never met anyone who looked forward to living somewhere that has mosquitoes; houses near water are guaranteed to be surrounded by midges and mosquitoes.

The further distant you are from civilisation, the more of nature you can expect to see. In a small village it's avoidable, in the middle of nowhere it's in your face. So if you don't like it, opt for a village or small town. Then at least there'll be neighbours to help you deal with it.

———

CONCLUSION

I hope you've found this book both illuminating and useful. Above all, I hope it hasn't deterred you from embarking on your dream of living in the country. For those of us drawn to a rural way of life it really can be vastly more satisfying than city living. I moved many years ago and have never once wanted to go back.

It is a whole different world out there, though. And the move will be far more satisfying and enjoyable if you know what the pitfalls are first so you can avoid them. Many people make the mistake of moving to the country without thinking through the consequences of the choices they make. This book should have helped you to learn from other people's mistakes so that, with sensible forethought, you can live a dream life in the country that meets all your expectations.

Useful contacts and addresses

There are plenty of organisations, businesses and advisory groups which you might find a useful information source if you're thinking of moving to the country. For example, the NRA (National Rivers Authority) may be able to tell you if the local river is prone to flooding, or the Society for the Preservation of Ancient Buildings could advise you about the best way to renovate an old property you're thinking of buying and doing up.

We have put together a list of all the organisations we can think of which might be useful. You can find this list on our website at www.whiteladderpress.com. Posting the list on the website means we can keep it updated. We also hope that you will let us know of any other organisations which we can add that you have found helpful in making the move.

IF YOU LIKE THIS BOOK, HOW ABOUT EARNING A FEW BOB RECOMMENDING IT TO OTHER PEOPLE?

We're looking for people who would like to earn a bit of extra cash, or maybe fundraise for a favourite charity, by helping to sell *Out of Your Townie Mind* or any of our other books.

The deal's very simple. If you're interested, we'll send you a handful of leaflets with an order form on the back. All you have to do is to mark them with your name and hand them out. Give them to friends, leave them in shops... we'll give you a few ideas to get you started. No need to do any hard selling if you're not comfortable with that. Then, for every order that comes back with your name on, we pay you a healthy commission. It's as simple as that. When you're ready for more leaflets, we'll send them to you.

If you want to know more, call Richard on 01803 814124. We'd love you to join us.

CONTACT US

You're welcome to contact White Ladder Press if you have any questions or comments for either us or the author. Please use whichever of the following routes suits you.

Phone 01803 813343 between 9am and 5.30pm

Email enquiries@whiteladderpress.com

Fax 01803 813928

Address: White Ladder Press, Great Ambrook, Near Ipplepen, Devon TQ12 5UL

Website www.whiteladderpress.com

KIDS&Co

"Ros Jay has had a brilliant idea, and what is more she has executed it brilliantly. **KIDS & CO** is the essential handbook for any manager about to commit the act of parenthood, and a thoroughly entertaining read for everyone else"
JOHN CLEESE

WHEN IT COMES TO RAISING YOUR KIDS, YOU KNOW MORE THAN YOU THINK.

So you spent five or ten years working before you started your family? Maybe more? Well, don't waste those hard-learned skills. Use them on your kids. Treat your children like customers, like employees, like colleagues.

No, really.

Just because you're a parent, your business skills don't have to go out of the window when you walk in throughthe front door. You may sometimes feel that the kids get the better of you every time, but here's one weapon you have that they don't: all those business skills you already have and they know nothing about. Closing the sale, win/win negotiating, motivational skills and all the rest.

Ros Jay is a professsional author who writes on both business and parenting topics, in this case simultaneously. She is the mother of three young children and stepmother to another three grown-up ones.

THE VOICE OF TOBACCO

"An amazing new book on smoking – it has great style and humour, and is brilliantly funny. Read this happy smoker's guide – if only I had been the author."
LESLIE PHILLIPS

What does the Voice of Tobacco say to you?
There's no need to give up; just cutting down will do.
How can it be bad for you when it feels so good?
Just one cigarette can't hurt you, now can it?
It's hard not to listen. Especially when, from the other side of the debate, we smokers have all been lectured by self-righteous prigs who think that (a) we should want to give up and (b) giving up smoking should be easy.
Well we don't and it ain't.
And yet there does come a time when, no matter how much we enjoy smoking, we have to become not smokers.
Richard Craze's guide gives it to you straight: what it's really like to give up smoking. The headaches, the sleeplessness, the irritability. And The Voice. He's been there and his diary reports back from the front line. It may not be pleasant, but it's honest. It may or may not help you to give up smoking, but it will certainly get you looking at smoking in a new way. And it will give you something to do with your hands.

This is the diary of a dedicated and happy smoker who is now not smoking. Here's how he did it. Here's how to do it without the trauma, the withdrawal symptoms, the twitching, the bad temper. Yeah, right. In your dreams.

The White Ladder Diaries

"To start a business from scratch with a great idea but little money is a terrifying but thrilling challenge. White Ladder is a fine example of how sheer guts and drive can win the day." **TIM WATERSTONE**

Have you ever dreamed of starting your own business?

Want to know what it's like? I mean, what it's really like?

Ros Jay and her partner, Richard Craze, first had the idea for White Ladder Press in the summer of 2002. This is the story of how they overcame their doubts and anxieties and brought the company to life, for only a few thousand pounds, and set it on its way to being a successful publishing company (this is its third book).

The White Ladder Diaries isn't all theory and recollections. It's a real life, day-by-day diary of all those crucial steps, naïve mistakes and emotional moments between conceiving the idea for a business and launching the first product. It records the thinking behind all the vital decisions, from choosing a logo or building a website, to sorting out a phone system or getting to grips with discounts.

What's more, the diary is littered with tips and advice for anyone else starting up a business. Whether you want to know how to register a domain name or how to write a press release, it's all in here.

If they could do it, so can you. Go on – stop dreaming. Be your own boss.

Babies for Beginners

If it isn't in here, you don't need to know it.

At last, here is the book for every new parent who's never been quite sure what a cradle cap is and whether you need one. **Babies for Beginners** cuts the crap – the unnecessary equipment, the over-fussy advice – and gives you the absolute basics of babycare: keep the baby alive, at all costs, and try to stop it getting too hungry.

From bedtime to bathtime, mealtime to playtime, this book highlights the CORE OBJECTIVE of each exercise (for example, get the baby bathed) and the KEY FOCUS (don't drown it). By exploding the myths around each aspect of babycare, the book explains what is necessary and what is a bonus; what equipment is essential and what you can do without.

Babies for Beginners is the perfect book for every first time mother who's confused by all the advice and can't believe it's really necessary to spend that much money. And it's the ultimate guide for every father looking for an excuse to get out of ante-natal classes.

Roni Jay is a professional author whose books include **KIDS & Co: winning business tactics for every family.** She is the mother of three young children, and stepmother to another three grown up ones.

ORDER FORM

You can order any of our books via any of the contact routes on page 146, including on our website. Or fill out the order form below and fax it or post it to us.

We'll normally send your copy out by first class post within 24 hours (but please allow five days for delivery). We don't charge postage and packing.

Title (Mr/Mrs/Miss/Ms/Dr/Lord etc) _____

Name _____

Address _____

_____

Postcode _____

Daytime phone number _____

Email _____

No. of copies	Title	Price	Total £
	TOTAL:		

Please either send us a cheque made out to White Ladder Press Ltd or fill in the credit card details below.

Type of card ☐ Visa ☐ Mastercard ☐ Switch

Card number _____

Start date (if on card) _____ Expiry date _____ Issue no (Switch) _____

Name as shown on card _____

Signature _____